Old Silltown, Something of Its History and People

MEMORABILIA
SARAH SILL WELLES BURT

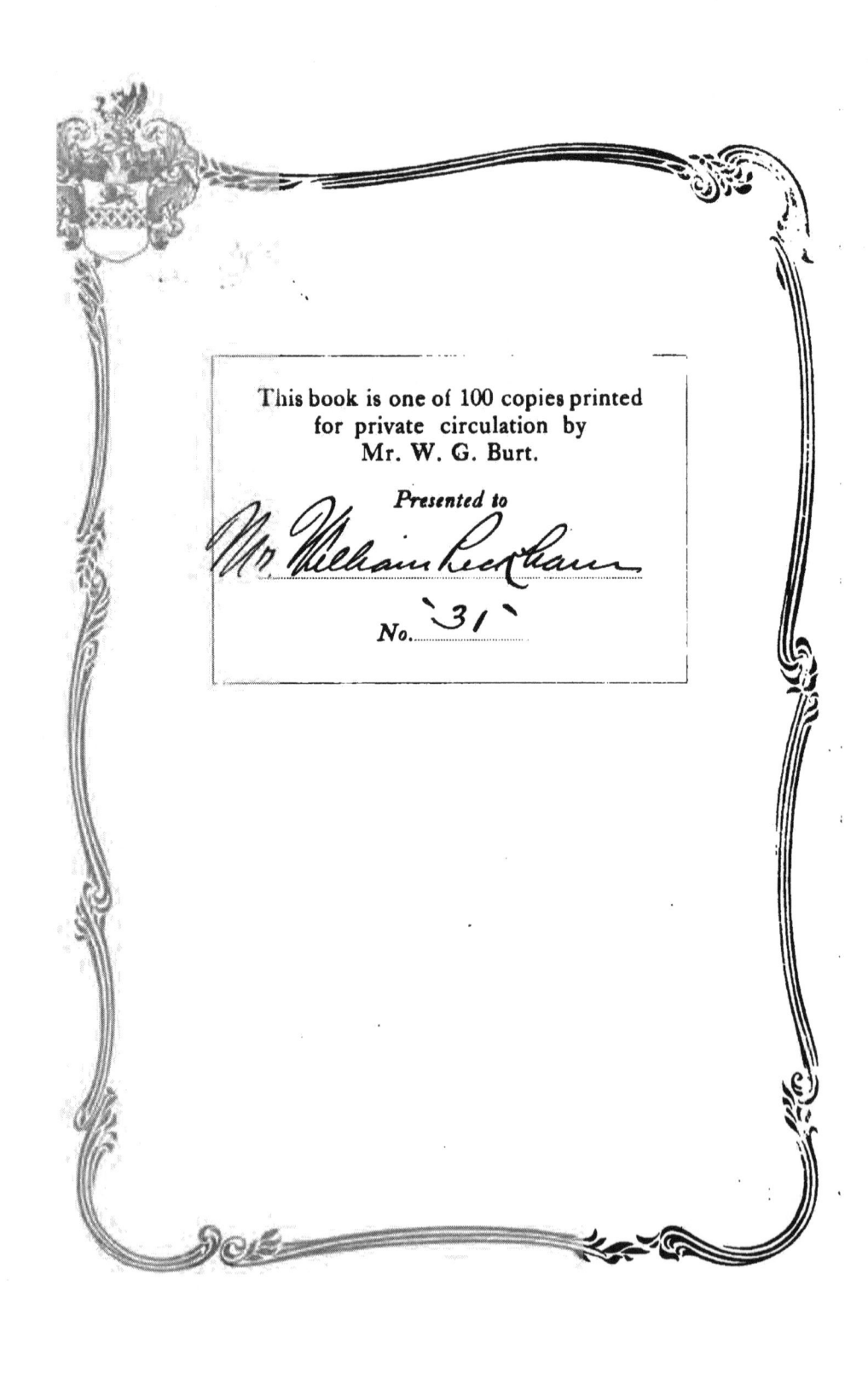

This book is one of 100 copies printed
for private circulation by
Mr. W. G. Burt.

Presented to

Mr. William Peckham

No. `31`

OLD SILLTOWN

SOMETHING OF ITS HISTORY AND PEOPLE

By

Sarah Sill Welles Burt

Great Grand-daughter of Lieutenant Colonel David Fithian Sill,
Grand-daughter of Captain Thomas Sill.

Being principally a brief account of the early
generations of the

SILL FAMILY

Their settlement in Connecticut and their accomplishments, gleanings
from old letters heretofore unpublished, early histories, reminiscences and traditions—also appreciations of those
decendants of recent generations who were well
known to the writer in their life time.

Copyright 1912
W. GRISWOLD BURT

In memory of my Progenitors

TO MY SON

WILLIAM GRISWOLD BURT

is

Inscribed this little volume

Sincerely yours,
Sarat W. Rust

Memorabilia

SARAH SILL WELLES BURT.

Sarah Sill Welles Burt, born in Utica, N. Y., in 1839, was the oldest daughter of Alfred Lee Welles and Sarah Griswold Sill, daughter of Captain Thomas Sill, of Lyme, Conn. (See Thomas Sill, Sixth Generation). Mr. Welles, her father, was for thirty years a prosperous merchant of Utica, a leading citizen of that city, and highly esteemed by the community.

The family residence at the time of the birth of Sarah Welles was located on Devereaux street, later on Broad street and, still later the family moved to a suburb of the city, Whitesboro, in order that Mr. Welles might be near to the Utica Cotton Mills, of which he at that time was proprietor.

The childhood education of Sarah Welles was acquired at a private school in Utica. At the age of fifteen, she was sent to the Maplewood Seminary at Pittsfield, Mass. Later she went with a friend (Sarah McCurdy Lord of Lyme) to the Spingler Institute of New York City, Fourteenth street and Broadway, conducted by Rev. Gorham D. Abbott (brother of John C. Abbott, the historian, and Uncle of Lyman Abbott, our present noted divine). Here, with much happiness, she acquired the finishing of her education. At that time her older brother, Thomas, was in Hamilton College, in the

MEMORABILIA

same class with the present Honorable Elihu Root. After the completion of her studies, and until her marriage, she divided her time quite equally between her aunt, Mrs. Mary Sill of Lyme, Conn., and her Utica home. It was thus by reason of such close association with and her love for her Aunt Mary that she came to so highly cherish and revere the traditions and memories of the old Sill family, and to love and respect so many of their friends amongst the Lyme people.

Previous to the death of Mrs. Mary Sill in 1903, Sarah Welles Burt came from her home in Chicago each season to spend part of the summer with Mrs. Mary Sill, and in later years to stay a few weeks at the Inn or Boxwood. Her old Lyme associations were always dear to her and she took a proud interest in the lives of its people, generations past and present. As a descendant of the old Sills, who had lived prosperously and honorably in the locality known as Silltown, who had faithfully served their community, state and country in civil and military capacities, she found pleasure in locating and acquiring the geneological data of the family and its connections, the stories and anecdotes of their lives and in doing what she could to preserve their traditions, relics and landmarks. The old Thomas Sill homestead, still standing in Silltown, where Mrs. Mary Sill lived and died, the old farm at the head of Lieutenant River with its boat landings and surrounding hills were scenes of her childhood that were always fresh in her mind and ever were the source of happiness in her memory.

In 1876 Sarah Welles was married to William Burt of Chicago, and for the remainder of her life resided in the city of Chicago itself or its North Shore suburb of Evanston.

MEMORABILIA

Her husband for thirty-five years was a well known business man, esteemed for ability and integrity, and beloved by men for the strength and force of his character. For the past twenty-nine years Sarah Welles Burt, with husband and son, resided in their Evanston residence. Mr. Burt, died of old age on June 6th, 1912, aged 84 years. For four years his wonderful New England constitution withstood the oncoming of the inevitable. During these trying years those who were close to Sarah Burt saw in the flesh the spirit of the Divine Master, whom she served. Seven weeks after the death of her husband, with whom she had for forty-five years trod the path of life, that Divine Master called her also to her everlasting rest.

>The Lord is my Shepherd
>He restoreth my Soul
>Though I walk through the valley of the shadow
>   of death I will fear no evil.

OBITUARY AS PUBLISHED IN THE INDEX OF EVANSTON, ILL., JULY 27TH, 1912.

Mrs. Sarah Welles Burt.

Mrs. Sarah Welles Burt, widow of William Burt, who for twenty-seven years, has been a resident of Evanston, died suddenly Sunday evening, July twenty-first, at the Mohican Hotel, New London, Conn., where she was stopping in expectation of proceeding to Old Lyme, Conn. Her remains were brought back to the Evanston home she so dearly loved where kind friends gave her their final earthly tributes.

MEMORABILIA

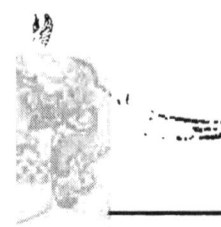

The funeral service Wednesday afternoon was conducted by her pastor, Rev. David Hugh Jones of the First Presbyterian church of this city and she was laid to rest at the side of her husband and children in the family lot in Graceland cemetery.

From the days of her girlhood she had derived much pleasure from oft repeated visits to the old New England home of friends and ancestors and was looking forward to her anticipated visit there this summer.

On Friday night an attack of acute indigestion induced by fatigued condition affected her heart. However by Saturday evening she was much better and on Sunday she was considered to be rapidly regaining her normal condition, but at seven fifteen o'clock Sunday evening during the hour of twilight her brave heart suddenly ceased to beat and her soul took flight to its Heavenly home.

Sarah Welles, born in Utica, N. Y., was the daughter of Alfred L. Welles, who for many years was a prosperous merchant of that city. Of the family two brothers still remain, Mr. George S. Welles of Park Ridge and Chicago, Ill., and Mr. Samuel M. Welles of Chicago. Sarah Welles, being the second child and oldest daughter of a family of ten children, many responsibilities fell to her. For the welfare of brothers and sisters she was ever mindful and after their death her deep affection continued unto their children.

In 1867 she was married to William Burt of Chicago, to whom she bore four children, first a son who died when eighteen months old and successively two baby daughters who died

MEMORABILIA

in earliest infancy, lastly a second son, Mr. W. Griswold Burt, who was with her at the time of her death.

Mrs. Burt survived the death of her husband by scarcely eight weeks. Never failing was her devotion to him during his four years of illness. As a daughter, as a sister, as a wife, as a mother her flow of sympathy was inexhaustible.

For those she loved no effort was too great, no service too small, no sorrow severe or trifling but that her devotion and sympathy went forth to alleviate it.

With a faith in her God and Saviour that was certain and unshakeable, with steadfast adherence to principle of rightness she fought the Battle of Life midst all circumstances with a smile on her face and a spirit that was brave. Truly could she have said

"I have fought a good fight,
I have kept the faith.
Henceforth there is laid up for me a crown of righteousness
Which the Lord the righteous judge shall give me at that day."

The death of Mrs. Sarah Welles Burt comes as a shock to all who knew her, especially to the friends who bade her good bye ten days ago at her departure in company with her son, on a visit to her old home in the East.

Mrs. Burt has been a member and regular attendant of the First Presbyterian church for the past twenty-two years and has always been interested in its various activities. In her church circle she leaves a vacancy which cannot be filled.

MEMORABILIA

She will also be missed at the gatherings of the University guild, of which she has been a member since its organization.

Mrs. Burt was a descendant of the Sill family on her mother's side and of the Welles on her father's. These families were among the early settlers of these states and figured prominently in their development. Being of this descent she was naturally interested in genealogical lore and historical events in connection with old New England, and especially in those events in which her forefathers were participants.

These associations led her to a keen interest in the organization of the Fort Dearborn chapter of the Daughters of the American Revolution of which she was a charter member. She has also been affiliated for many years with the Chicago chapter.

Mrs. Burt was a woman of rare refinement and delicacy, of high intellectual qualities,—capable, sympathetic, gracious. As her pastor, Mr. Jones, stated at her funeral service, there are heroes in life, who endure burdens with fortitude and reserve, and as truly give their lives for others as do the heroes of the battle-field. Mrs. Burt was one of these, assuming with uncomplaining cheerfulness and unswerving fidelity all demands which the circumstances of life made upon her. Amidst many exacting duties, she found time to think and act for others. Many were her deeds of kindness and thoughtfulness which endeared her to her neighbors and friends. By these her loss is deeply grieved; by these she will be sorely missed; among these her memory will linger long, for to know her was to love her.

MEMORABILIA

GENEALOGY OF SARAH SILL WELLES BURT, AS DESCENDANT OF JOHN SILL OF ENGLAND.

Sarah Sill Welles Burt, daughter of
Alfred L. Welles and Sarah Griswold Sill, daughter of
Mahitable Mather and Thomas Sill, son of
Sarah Griswold and David Fithian Sill, son of
Phoebe Fithian and Lieutenant John Sill, son of
Phoebe Lord and Joseph Sill the 2nd, son of
Sarah Marvin Clark and Joseph Sill the 1st, son of
John Sill of England.

MEMORABILIA

GENEALOGY OF SARAH SILL WELLES BURT, AS DESCENDANT OF GEORGE CLARK.

George Clark (1610-1690), among the original proprietors of the town of Milford, Connecticut, Deputy to General Court of Connecticut—1666.

Sarah Sill Welles Burt, daughter of
Alfred L. Welles and Sarah Griswold Sill, daughter of
Mahitable Mather and Captain Thomas Sill, son of
Sarah Griswold and Captain David Fithian Sill, son of
Phoebe Fithian and Lieutenant John Sill, son of
Phoebe Lord and Joseph Sill the 2nd, son of
Joseph Sill the 1st, and Sarah Clark, daughter of
George Clark, of Milford, Connecticut.

MEMORABILIA

GENEALOGY OF SARAH SILL WELLES BURT, AS DESCENDANT OF JUDGE NATHANIAL LYNDE.

Sarah Sill Welles Burt, daughter of
Alfred Welles and Sarah Griswold Sill, daughter of
Mahitable Mather and Thomas Sill, son of
David Fithian Sill and Sarah Griswold, daughter of
Thomas Griswold and Susanna Lynde, daughter of
Sarah Pratt and Nathanial Lynde, son of
Susanna Willouby and Judge Nathanial Lynde, son of
Hannah Newdigate and Simon Lynde, son of
Elizabeth Digby (related to Earl of Windsor) and Enoch Lynde (of England).

NOTE.—Lieutenant William Pratt died 1678, early settler of Saybrook, Conn., Deputy from Saybrook to General Court of Connecticut twenty-three times, Soldier in Pequot War 1637, County Magistrate in 1666, Lieutenant of Saybrook Band Oct. 3d, 1661. See Connecticut Colonial Records, Pratt, General.

Hartford in the Olden Times, pp. 117.
Hinman's Early Settlers.
Bodgés Soldiers of King Phillip's War.

MEMORABILIA

GENEALOGY OF SARAH SILL WELLES BURT, AS DESCENDANT OF THOMAS LEE (OR LEIGH).

Sarah Sill Welles Burt, daughter of
Sarah Griswold Sill and Alfred Lee Welles, son of
Alfred Welles and Abigail Lee, daughter of
Betsy Elizabeth Smith and Seth Lee, son of
Hepzibah Lee and Elisha Lee, son of
Elizabeth Graham and Thomas Lee.

Thomas Lee was representative to the General Court from Lyme sixteen times and repeatedly Justice of the Peace.

Elisha Lee (above mentioned), born in 1714, served in the Indian Wars as paymaster. A great-grand-daughter of his writes that Elisha Lee, having been captured by the Indians and sentenced to be burned at the stake, a friendly Indian took him on his back at midnight when there was snow on the ground, carried him to a river and leaving him, returned alone. As only one set of foot prints, and those an Indian's, were to be seen the white man could cross the river without being traced, which he did.

MEMORABILIA

GENEALOGY OF SARAH SILL WELLES BURT, AS DESCENDANT OF REV. RICHARD MATHER OF ENGLAND.

Rev. Richard Mather of England married Catharine Holt
    their son
Timothy Mather married Catharine Atherton
    their son
Richard Mather married Catharine Wise
    their son
Samuel Mather married Deborah Champion
    their son
Richard Mather married Deborah Ely
    their son
Samuel Mather married Lois Griswold
    their daughter
Mahitable Mather married Thomas Sill
    their daughter
Sarah Griswold Sill married Alfred L. Welles.
    and
Sarah Sill Welles was their daughter.

NOTE.—Rev. Richard Mather came to this country in the vessel Angel Gabrial, born in Lancashire, England, 1596, was schoolmaster at Toxeth Park, near Liverpool, at the age of fifteen; studied at Braymore College, Oxford; 1618 was ordained in the English Church and became Minister of Toxeth, in which position he remained fifteen years. He was suspended for non-conformity to the ceremonies of the Established Church in 1633. He therefore emigrated to New England, arriving in Boston in 1635; the next year he became pastor of the church in Dorchester and remained in that position until his death, 1669. He was one of the compilers of the Bay Book Psalms. (See Mather Genealogy and Savage's Genealogy and History.)

MEMORABILIA

GENEALOGY OF SARAH SILL WELLES BURT, AS DESCENDANT OF MAJOR GENERAL HUMPHREY ATHERTON.

Catharine Atherton (daughter of Humphrey Atherton) married Timothy Mather,
> their son

Richard Mather married Catharine Wise
> their son

Samuel Mather married Deborah Champion
> their son

Richard Mather married Deborah Ely
> their son

Samuel Mather married Lois Griswold
> their daughter

Mahitable Mather married Thomas Sill,
> their daughter

Sarah Sill married Alfred Welles
> and

Sarah Sill Welles was their daughter

MEMORABILIA

GENEALOGY OF SARAH SILL WELLES BURT, AS DESCENDANT OF DEPUTY GOVERNOR FRANCIS WILLOUBY.

William Willouby of Portsmouth, Hampshire, England,
    his son
Francis Willouby married Margaret Locke Taylor (2nd cousin to Queen Elizabeth of England). He was Deputy Governor of Massachusetts from 1665 to 1675.
    their daughter
Susanna Willouby married Judge Nathanial Lynde
    their son
Nathaniel Lynde married Sarah Pratt
    their daughter
Susanna Lynde married Thomas Griswold
    their daughter
Sarah Griswold married David Fithian Sill
    etc., etc. (See Genealogy by Greenwood-Frothingham's History Wallinghampshire.)

NOTE.—William Willouby was commissioner of the British Navy from 1648 to 1651, when he died. His son, Francis Willouby, came to New England in 1638 and returned to England in 1651. In 1652 he was appointed successor to his father as commissioner of the navy, and in 1658 chosen member of parliament from Portsmouth. In 1662 he returned to New England and became Deputy Governor of the Massachusetts Colony in 1665 and continued so until his death in 1675.

MEMORABILIA

GENEALOGY OF SARAH SILL WELLES BURT, AS DESCENDANT OF MATTHEW GRISWOLD OF ENGLAND.

Matthew Griswold of Warwickshire (Kennelworth, native place) married Anna Wolcot.
> their son

Matthew (born 1653, died 1699, representative for Saybrook often, and for Lyme after division of the town in 1667) married Phoebe Hyde
> their son

Judge John Griswold married Hannah Leigh
> their son

Thomas Griswold (brother of Gov. Matthew Griswold) married Mary Lee
> their son

Thomas Griswold married Susanna Lynde
> their daughter

Sarah Griswold married David Fithian Sill,
> etc., etc. (See Savage, Sill and Mather Genealogies.)

Preface to Old Silltown

The contents of this book were collected and arranged by Sarah Sill Welles Burt at the expense of much time and patient effort. It was her expectation to have them put into book form in order that the descendants of the old Sill family might thus have the data compact and systematically arranged, that their children and their children's children might thus the more readily become familiar with the record of their honorable ancestors and themselves be inspired to lead lives worthy of such noble progenitors. Owing to the sudden death of Sarah Sill Welles Burt this was not accomplished in her lifetime, but that her efforts may not have been in vain, her purpose has, in this volume, to the extent of his ability, been carried out by her son, W. Griswold Burt.

This volume is not intended as a complete genealogy of the Sill family. The reader will note that parts of the contents are in the nature of personal expressions of appreciation and love for those mentioned. The incidents herein related concern only a very small proportion of the descendants, and are recorded here by reason of their special interest to those living in this present time. Thus many who have left records of good and useful lives remain unmentioned here. The writer is indebted to many sources of information for what is related here.

OLD SILLTOWN

Many of the items were made memorandum of after hearing them told by living lips, many of whom have now gone to their everlasting rest. Also certain books and records have served as authority among which may be mentioned:
Connecticut Records 1678, Sq., pp. 195-208-211.
Connecticut Records 1689, Sq., pp. 23-33-42-69.
General Gookins' History of the Praying Indians.
Hubbard's Narration of the Indian Wars in New England.
Page's History of Cambridge.
Increase Mather's History of King Phillip's War.
George Bodge's Soldiers of King Phillip's Wars.
Sill Family Genealogy, by George G. Sill and Louisa P. Sill.
Trumbull's History of Connecticut.
Old Letters—deeds, Inventories of Estates, etc.
Knox's Campaigns.
Connecticut Records at Smithsonian Institute, Washington, D. C.
Shurtleft's History of Boston.
Orcult's History of Dorchester.
Salisbury's History and Genealogy.
Connecticut Colonial Records at Hartford.
Matthew's American Armory and Blue Book.
Sill-Treadway Genealogy, by F. S. Sill.
Genealogy of the Loomis Family.
Hyde Genealogy.
Ancient Windsor, Connecticut, by H. R. Stiles.
Oneida Historical Society Transactions.
Savage's Genealogy Dictionary.

Incentivus

"Our ancestors, a gallant Christian race of every virtue, every grace."

* * * *

"—There is also a moral and philosophical respect for our ancestors, which elevates the character and improves the heart.—"
—Daniel Webster.

* * * *

The Divine command to "remember the days of old and consider the years of many generations" (Deut. 32-7), so oft repeated in varying terms in Holy Writ, is an imperative argument for the preservation of memorials of the past.

SILL COAT OF ARMS.

MOTTO---TAM FIDUS QUAM FIXUS
"EQUALLY FAITHFUL AS STEADFAST."

OLD SILLTOWN

Crest

A DEMI GRIFFIN RAMPANT PROPER COLLARD ARGENT

> A demi—(one-half) griffin—Symbol of a guardian of treasure, or one entrusted.
>
> Rampant—Showing courage and generosity.
>
> Proper—i. e.—colored like a mythical griffin, bronze, green and glistening.
>
> Collard argent—silver—(honor and clear conscience).

Arms

ARGENT—A FEASE ENGRAVED SABLE IN CHIEF
"A LION RAMPANT PASSING GULES."

> Argent—Silver, symbolizing honor or a clear conscience.
>
> A fesse engrailed—Indicating the sash or belt of a commander.
>
> Sable—black—Meaning fame.
>
> In chief—or top part of shield.
>
> A lion—Signifying courage, majesty and strength.
>
> Rampant passing—or progressive.
>
> Gules—Red, the royal color, denoting zeal.

CHAPTER I.

LOCATION OF SILLTOWN.

In New London County, Connecticut, on the road leading from North Lyme and Hamburg to Old Lyme, there lies beneath the hills an especially charming and fertile valley, embracing a few hundred acres.

Its western boundary is Lieutenant River, whose source is amidst the hills and whose waters (about a mile and a half farther south) mingle with those of the Connecticut River before its entrance to Long Island Sound.

At the east and south of this attractive valley is Mill Creek, which, in its turn, flows into the Lieutenant River, and thus serves as an outlet for the Great Lake farther north, now called Roger's Lake.

From the Old Lyme Station of the New York, New Haven and Hartford Railroad this locality may be reached by driving up the main street of Old Lyme, taking the North Road, where it diverges from the New London turnpike, when on crossing Mill Creek bridge at the foot of the hill one arrives at its southern boundary.

For generations this locality has been known as Silltown.

It was on this tract of land, nearly surrounded by hills, that Captain Joseph Sill settled more than two hundred and fifty years ago. He was the son of John Sill of England (First Generation).

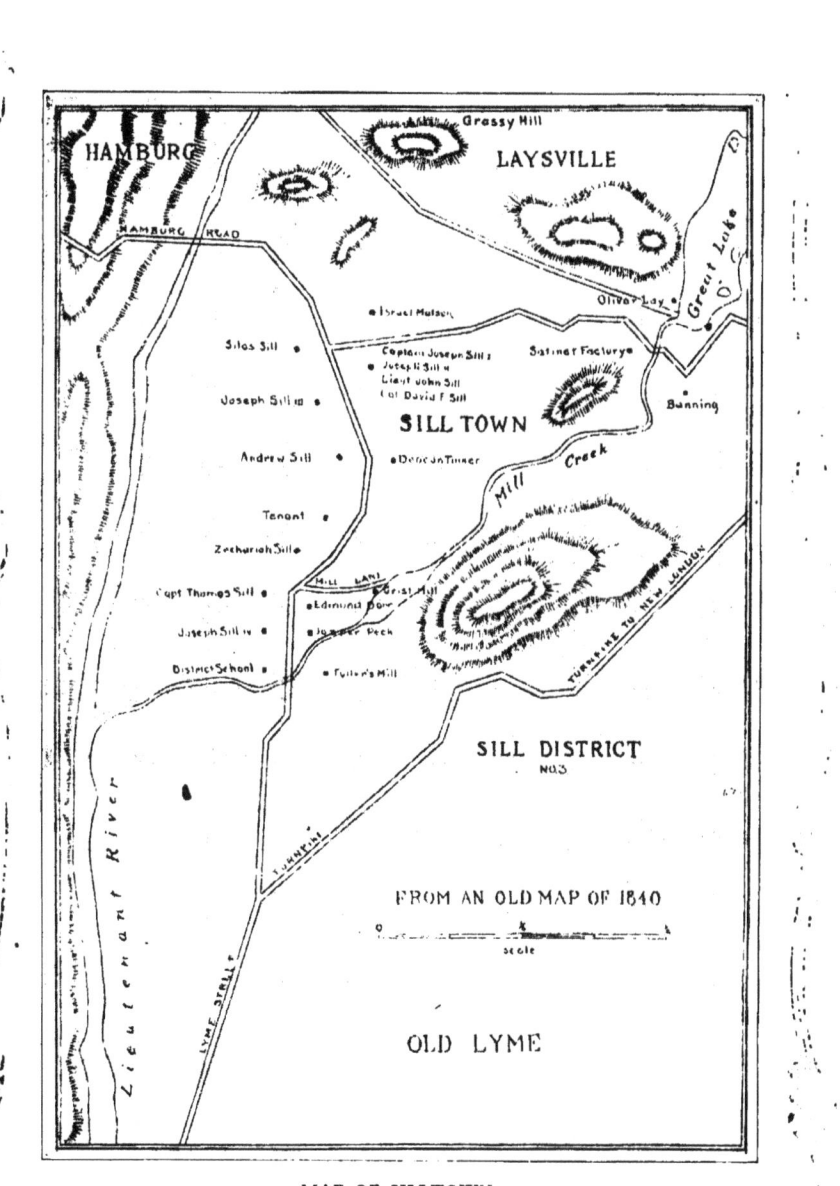

MAP OF SILLTOWN.

First Generation

JOHN SILL OF ENGLAND.

John Sill of England came to this country with his family in the year 1637 and settled in Cambridge, Massachusetts, about eighteen years after the landing of the Pilgrims at Plymouth, seven years after the settlement of Cambridge was commenced, and the same year in which Harvard College was founded.

Mr. Sill was admitted to the privileges of a freeman at Cambridge in the year 1638, and was received as member in full communion of the Congregational Society of Cambridge, Rev. Thomas Shepherd pastor.

The earliest genealogist of the family, Henry A. Sill, of Cuyahoga Falls, has stated that a tradition in the family was that John Sill came from Lyme Regis, Dorchestershire, England. History states this to have been a seaport town located on the Linn River, a summer resort of the kings of England, a royal manor from the time of Edward the First, and a place mentioned in history from "The Doomsday Book" onward.

The eldest daughter of John Sill, born and baptized in England, was Elizabeth, born in 1637, married Zachariah Hicks in 1652, died in 1736, according to the gravestone still standing in Cambridge.

A second daughter, born in Cambridge, Mass., married Abraham Shepherd, of Malden, Mass.

OLD SILLTOWN

In 1838 John Sill owned property at the corner of Eliot and Winthrop streets, and in 1842 he owned a house and several acres of land, and in 1845 he had an additional grant of land. He was living in 1647, when he was among the creditors of a certain estate, and in 1648-9 he was named among the proprietors of land in Cambridge, but he died before 1652, for at that time his wife is spoken of as a widow. It is probable that his birth took place in about 1610, in the early years of James the First. (See Sill-Treadway Gen., by Frederick S. Sill.)

Mrs. Joanna Sill survived her husband about twenty years. She received allotments of land in 1652. (See Paige's History of Cambridge.) Her will was presented for probate in 1671, so she probably died in that year. (See Sill-Treadway Genealogy.)

The year in which this young emigrant, John Sill, and his wife, Joanna with infant children, came to New England was the one in which John Hampden was condemned for resisting the levying of ship money. It may well have been that they were induced to leave their English home by reason of the persecutions which arose at that time, and the trouble, which between 1630 and 1640, had led, as Green says, to the sailing of two hundred emigrant ships with twenty thousand Englishmen, who sought a refuge in the West.

Charles the First was then king, and William Laud Archbishop of Canterbury.

Milton was the poet of the day.

The Earl of Strafford was Prime Minister.

It was seventeen years before Oliver Cromwell became Lord Protector of England, and twelve before the death of

OLD SILLTOWN

Charles. It was the time of great political and religious changes, which materially aided the success of the settlement of New England. (See Sill-Treadway Gen.)

CHAPTER II.

Second Generation

JOSEPH SILL, THE FIRST.

Captain Joseph, the only son of John Sill the 1st, was born in England in 1636, married, in 1660, Jemina Belcher, a niece of Lieutenant-Governor Thomas Danford, of Massachusetts, also aunt to Governor Johnathan Belcher of the same state.

Sons— 1 Andrew
2 Joseph
3 Andrew
4 Thomas
Daughters— 5 Jemina
6 Elizabeth.

Of these several children born to them two sons are supposed to have been lost at sea, others were married and left descendants. However, the name of Sill became extinct in Massachusetts after Joseph, the first removed to Connecticut. His wife died in 1675. He later became actively engaged in the defense of the colonies, in the suppression of the Northern Indians.

The public records found in the Newberry Library of Chicago, Illinois, published by the order of the General Court of Massachusetts, states that, "On the roster of officers of the first American army as organized for the Narragansett Colony, mustered at Pettiguamscot, December 19th, 1665, (General Josiah Winslow, Governor of Plymouth Colony, Commander in Chief), was the name of Captain Joseph Sill.

OLD SILLTOWN

A partial record of his service states that at the outbreak of King Phillip's War in 1675 he was a lieutenant.

In September of that year he was commissioned Captain of one hundred men under Major Pynchon. In November, by order of the Court, he was commissioned Captain of a company raised at Charleston, Watertown and Cambridge. During the whole of this war he rendered valuable service to the colonies and was engaged in numerous expeditions, being sent as far as Saco, Maine. Among his most famous exploits was one at Lancaster, February 21st, in 1675, where he captured three hundred Indians, and another where he conducted a long train of wagons, bringing the inhabitants of Groton to Boston is safety with a single company of troopers, fifty in all, successfully resisting the attacks of the Indians along the route.

The war closed when King Phillip, that brave son of Massasoit, was massacred on August 12th, 1676, by one of his own followers while hiding from his enemies in the marshes. This locality, near South Kingston, Rhode Island, where the fiercest and most decisive battle was fought, where history states a thousand Indians were killed and their stronghold demolished, has in recent years been marked with a granite monument by the inhabitants of the town that the event may be commemorated and the locality designated for future generations. The monument is visible at a distance, and can be seen from the train when passing from Providence to Boston, via the Shore Line of the New York, New Haven and Hartford Railroad. The first attention of the passerby is attracted to this locality by signs on the roadside which read thus: "The Great Swamp Fight."

OLD SILLTOWN

In an old volume, "History of America," by Henry Trumbull, published in Norwich in 1810, copy owned by Mr. Daniel Ingraham Lay, is recorded on page 62 as follows:

"On the 12th of December, 1679, a party of Indians attacked and killed several of the inhabitants of Bradford. The Governor of Massachusetts Colony, for the protection and defense of the inhabitants on the Merrimack, ordered the raising and equipping of four companies of cavalry, to the command of which were appointed Captains Sill, Holyoke, Cutler and Prentis." Thus showing that Captain Sill was called in emergencies to come into the service of the colony in command of horse as well as foot soldiers. The historical records of his service are too lengthy for more than reference here. They may be found in Hubbard's Narrative of the Indian Wars in New England, Paige's History of Cambridge, Mass., in Gen. Gookin's History of Praying Indians, and especially in George M. Bodge's Soldiers of King Phillips' War.

Influenced by his friends, who feared lest he might become the victim of the vengeance of the remaining Indians, Captain Sill removed from the Narragansett to the Connecticut Colony. Before leaving Massachusetts he appealed to the General Court of that colony for a grant of land; the original, ably drawn petition is in possession of the Boston Historical Society.

George Bodge in his volume, Soldiers of King Phillip's War, has introduced a copy of this document as follows:

OLD SILLTOWN

"TO THE HONORABLE GENERAL COURT, ASSEMBLED AT BOSTON, THE PETITION OF JOSEPH SILL HUMBLY SHOWETH, VIZ:

"that your petitioner accounts it a great privilege that, from his childhood he hath been trained up and hath spent so many of his days under your government, and cannot without singular content and complacency, call to mind that he hath been honored to be called forth under your commission to appear in the field against your enemies in pursuance of which he did accordingly to his mean ability serve you faithfully and for length of time and number of expeditions, may (without ostentation be it spoken) compare with most if not any who were listed in your service, and accounts no part of his days, next to those which have been improved in the immediate service of God, so well spent as those which have been employed in the service of his country and the government, remaining still, devoted in all that he hath and still in your service without any selfish aims. Yet being well assured that your noble and generous inclinations are not inferior to his who accounted that day lost in which some one or other were not benefitted by him nor to his who was displeased with such as asked no kindness from him, he must confess that he hath some ambition that it may be manifested that he is not forgotten amongst those that have tasted of your beneficence and humbly craves of the honored court that you would please grant him a small number of acres of that land which hath been recovered from the enemy so that a little

OLD SILLTOWN

part of what he hath seen with his eyes and trod with his feet in your service, may be committed into his hands, and that he may the more comfortably share in the blessing of these peaceful days wherein man may beat their swords into plow shares, and your petitioners shall pray, etc., etc."

Joseph Sill.

The Court granted to him the tract of land where now is located the town of Salem. This was inherited by his daughter Jemima, who married John Hall of Medford, whose descendants are now living.

His removal to Lyme occurred about the time of the division of Saybrook, which had occupied both sides of the Connecticut River near its confluence with the Sound. Joseph Sill, coming, as tradition states, from Lyme Regis, England, and being a landed proprietor, he probably had an influence in giving the town the name of Lyme. The settlement of the locality commenced in about 1664, and in about 1667 the town was incorporated, having thirty families, and able to support a minister. The community had enjoyed the services of Rev. Mr. Noyes from 1666, but no church was organized until 1693, there not previously having been sufficient members to constitute a church. Mr. Noyes died in 1729, aged 86 years, having spent 63 years with his people. (See Trumbull's History of Connecticut and Sill Genealogy.)

In 1677 Capt. Joseph Sill married his second wife, Sarah Clark Marvin, the widow of Lieutenant Renolds Marvin. She was the daughter of George Clark, of Millford, Conn.,

OLD SILLTOWN

one of the early settlers of that town, who erected a massive stone bridge, which still bears his name.

In an old volume entitled "Colonial History," by John W. Barber, published in New Haven, 1830, in page 231 Joseph Sill is recorded as having been appointed AFTER PLANTER in the town of Millford, Conn. By the term PLANTER was meant one holding property, and consequently being recorded as being entitled to a voice in town affairs. The prefix AFTER meaning that other people had been recorded before him.

Captain Sill erected his home in Lyme on one of the hills overlooking his farm, having an extended view of the surrounding country, and a distant view of the Connecticut River and Long Island Sound.

The tax records for those early years, 1677, found in the archives of the Newberry Library of Chicago, give Mr. Sill's list to be as follows:

"Two persons	1 yearling
housing and lands	10 swine
6 oxen	3 geldings
12 cows	2 yearlings
7 horses	Lbs. 143—1406 being 1 per
1 gelding	cent.

The grist mills on Mill Lane, and saw mill in Laysville, important plants in those days, 1688, in which Captain Sill was interested, were managed by him and his descendants. Colonel David Fithian Sill of the fifth generation, being principal owner in them, as the inventory of his estate records.

OLD SILLTOWN

Aside from his farming interests, Joseph Sill was a promoter of the interests of the town. He was frequently elected

THE GRIST MILL.

to office in Connecticut and was deputy to the General Court

MILL POND.

several times in 1686, 1691 and 1693. He held commissions in both Connecticut and Massachusetts.

OLD SILLTOWN

Captain Joseph Sill was sixty years of age at the time of his death, which occurred October 6, 1696. His widow survived him nineteen years. Savage, the genealogist and historian, calls him "The distinguished officer," "The Fierce Indian Fighter." George Bodge, compiler and editor of "Soldiers of King Phillip's Wars," devotes an entire chapter to his service in the Colonial Wars.

I give here his quaint old signature in 1688, taken from an ancient document in the town record at Hamburg, Conn., traced by William Marvin, town clerk, from the original as found upon old records in connection with a town distribution of land.

In the early records of the Congregational Society of Old Lyme frequent mention is made of Joseph Sill, and in the Old Lyme town records of early times, now kept in Hamburg, are recorded transactions with Joseph Sill in transfer of land, etc. In town meeting book, under date of March 6, 1676, Captain Sill is recorded as one of three appointed to run the town bounds between Lyme and Haddam.

The following is taken from a letter written at Lyme, Conn., September 28, 1910, and signed by William Marvin, Judge of Probate, Town Clerk:

"The highway which leads past the former residence of Colonel Matson was not laid out until 1719, but at that time Joseph Sill, Jr., owned land adjoining it on the south. It is probable that Joseph Sill, Sr., owned this land before his death; it is certain that he owned land east of the main highway, north of the millstream and an interest in the corn and saw mill, which were very important plants in those early days, for the carrying on of which he was given special grants by the town. Joseph Sill, Sr., was not as large a land holder as his sons, Joseph and Zachariah, who gradually pur-

GRAVE OF JOSEPH SILL THE FIRST.
A Marble Slab Above His Tomb with Record of Service.

chased all of the lands north of the millstream, east of the Lieutenant River and southwest of the highway, as well as a tract east of the highway, stretching nearly from the millstream to the Matson cross road. They also owned lands, now held by Robert Hall, on the north shore of Lieutenant River, as well as tracts on Grassy Hill and Beaver River."

OLD SILLTOWN

To those familiar with the country around Old Lyme and Silltown the principal point of interest in the above quotation is contained in the last sentence, which shows that Captain Joseph Sill's holdings in lands included part of that region now known as the Billy Coult Hills.

Third Generation

Third Generation	Second Generation	First Generation
Joseph Sill, 2nd		John Sill
Phoebe Lord	Joseph Sill, 1st	of
Zachariah Sill	Sarah Clark Marvin	England
Elizabeth Mather		

Captain Joseph Sill, the first settler, by his second marriage had two sons named Joseph 2nd and Zachariah, who were 18 and 14 years of age respectively at the time of their father's death. Rev. George Griswold Sill, another historian and genealogist of the family, has called them, in a letter to his cousins preserved by the family, "The Patriarchs or "Heads" of branches of the family.

From these are descended all the Sills of this country as far as are now known. Joseph had twelve children, Zachariah six.

Eighteen children of the name of Sill in the neighborhood at one time was not unusual, and the same genealogist says of these: "Like the Israelites of old, not a feeble one among them." Their homes were erected about sixty rods apart in Silltown, while some of the later generations built farther down the street. The number of families of this name, in what was originally the town of Lyme, was eight or ten. This locality was then first called Silltown.

The nine sons of these two branches first settled in Silltown, some removing later to other settlements, North Lyme, Grassy Hill, Saybrook, Middletown, Windsor, Groton and other towns in Connecticut.

Joseph 2nd and Zachariah were more extensive land owners than their father before them, having large holdings

OLD SILLTOWN

in Grassy Hill and in different parts of Lyme, also in Ohio on Beaver River.

Joseph 2nd lived for thirty years in the home of his father, when he purchased improved lands in North Lyme and removed thither in 1733, leaving the homestead to his oldest son, Lieutenant John Sill. Joseph Sill was a member of the Congregational Church under the ministry of Rev. Moses Noyes of Lyme. He died in 1765, aged 88 years.

Joseph 2nd, married Phoebe Lord, daughter of Lieutenant Richard Lord of Lyme. Their children were:

Sons—
    John
    Joseph
    Thomas
    Jabez
    Richard
    Elijah
    Elisha

Daughters—
    Luce
    Elizabeth
    Phoebe
    Lucy
    Sarah

Zachariah 1st married Elizabeth Mather, daughter of Richard Mather of Lyme, niece of Increase Mather of Boston, President of Harvard College. Their children were:

OLD SILLTOWN

Sons—Andrew
Zachariah
David
Daughters— Sarah
Elizabeth
Johanna

The descendants of the two sons (Joseph 2nd and Zachariah) intermarried with families in Lyme, the Lords, Matsons, Noyes, Mathers, Griswolds, Lays and others.

OLD SILLTOWN

DESCENDANTS OF JOSEPH SILL THE SECOND.
Fourth Generation

First Generation	Second Generation	Third Generation	Fourth Generation
John Sill of England	Joseph Sill 1st	Joseph Sill 2nd	John Sill Joseph, 3rd Thomas Jabez Richard Elijah Elijah Luce Elizabeth Phoebe Lucy Sarah

LIEUTENANT JOHN SILL.

Lieutenant John, born in 1710, the eldest son of Joseph 2nd, inherited of his father the home on the hill. He was an owner of vessels, and when trading along the coast must then have met his first wife (he had three). In this way at least G. G. Sill, the historian, accounts for his marrying his first wife, Phoebe Fithian, of Bridgehampton, Long Island.

He passed much of his life on the farm where he was born. He was a man much loved and respected, was patriotic and loyal, and recorded as being a member of the "trained band," which no doubt answered to the militia of the present day.

Lieutenant John Sill was appointed Lieutenant of the first company or "trained band" in the town of Lyme in October, 1758, by the Colonial Assembly (see Colonial Records of Connecticut, 1757-1762, page 209), and is an acceptable ancestor to the "Colonial Society." He died in 1796, aged 86 years.

OLD SILLTOWN

He was a member of the Congregational Church for sixty-three years, having united in 1733, during the ministry of Johnathan Parsons.

His second and third wives were Hepzibah Lee and Lucy Peck. There were ten children, six sons and four daughters.

Sons—
David Fithian
Joseph 4th
John 3rd
Silas
Enoch
Richard

Daughters—
Phoebe
Mary
Anna
Sarah

"Some of these sons were to become famous and take a part in the Revolutionary War; indeed daughters, as well as sons, had something to do to help on with the War of Independence."

JOSEPH SILL THE THIRD.

Joseph 3rd, second son of Joseph 2nd, erected his home across the street from his fathers. His first wife was Ruth Matson, a neighbor's daughter. His second wife Azubah Lee, in some manner never accounted for, contracted smallpox, which resulted in her death. Ten years later her husband died of the same disease in a manner equally mysterious. Their graves laid side by side in the lot adjoining the one where their home once stood, the spot marked by tablets with inscriptions thereon. In 1910 these stones were removed to the Sill lot in Lyme cemetery, the fourth generation of Sills thus being represented in the old Sill burying ground in Old Lyme. Their children were Giles, Nathaniel, William, Joseph Lee, Rheubana, Lucy, Ruth, Phoebe, Azubah, Phoebe.

THOMAS SILL, FOURTH GENERATION.

Thomas Sill, third son of Joseph Sill the 2nd, settled in Grassy Hill.

RICHARD SILL, FOURTH GENERATION.

Richard Sill, fifth son of Joseph Sill the 2nd, settled in Saybrook.

JABEZ SILL, FOURTH GENERATION.

Jabez Sill, fourth Son of Joseph Sill the 2nd, settled in North Lyme.

Elisha and Elijah Sill, the youngest sons of Joseph 2nd, were graduates of Yale College. Elijah graduated in 1748. He studied theology and became a Congregational clergyman, and settled at New Fairfield, Connecticut. Elisha graduated in 1764. In 1777 Elisha was surgeon in General Wolcot's brigade of Connecticut Volunteers. He was present at the capture of Burgoyne's army at Saratoga. He was one of the magistrates of Litchfield, Conn., for many years, dying at the age of 78 years.

OLD SILLTOWN

Savage, the genealogist and historian, states that eight of this enterprising family were graduates of Yale College, then located on the shores of Long Island Sound at Saybrook. The early history of Yale College, as published in 1893, by Harper Brothers, in "Histories of the Four Prominent Universities," is of interest.

It states, "Yale was founded at the beginning of the last century along the shores of Long Island Sound. For many years it was difficult to say what it was or where it belonged. It was a "Collegeiate School" and was established (Dr. Cary states in his "Historic Memorial Discourse of the First Congregational Church of Lyme," in 1870) by a young man, Rev. James Pierpont of New Haven. The General Assembly of Connecticut was afraid to attract the notice of England to any undertaking of this kind. Such notice would have cost the college its charter. Its teaching force did not at first receive the names of President and Professor, but was obliged to content itself with Rector and Tutor. The Rector lived at Milford, the Tutors, at Saybrook; the senior class at the former place, and the professors' class at the latter. It was not till the removal of the school to New Haven in 1706 that it successfully attained a local habitation and a name."

OLD SILLTOWN

DESCENDANTS OF JOSEPH SILL, THE SECOND, THROUGH HIS FIRST SON, JOHN SILL.

Fifth Generation

DAVID FITHIAN SILL.

David Fithian Sill, oldest son of Lieutenant John Sill, served his country at intervals over a period of twenty-one years. He was born in 1733, and served in the French and Indian Wars. He received a commission from Governor Fitch, of Connecticut, in 1759 as lieutenant in the reign of of George Second, and was in service on Lake George and at Crown Point, and took the first French prisoner at the opening of the campaign. In 1760 he reinlisted in the army, went up the Mohawk River with Lord Amherst and to Oswego, from thence to Oswegatchie (now Ogdensburg), was with Commodore Loring on board the Onondaga at the attack on Isle Royal. He descended the St. Lawrence River with the army to Montreal, where the French surrendered to Lord Amherst. The war closed and Lieutenant David Fithian Sill returned to his native town.

He then married, in 1760, Sarah Griswold, daughter of Deacon Thomas Griswold, brother of Governor Matthew Griswold, of Black Hall, Conn. Her mother was Susanna Lynde, of Saybrook, daughter of Judge Nathaniel Lynde. In an article recently published on the treasurers of Yale College, it was stated that Judge Lynde was the first treasurer of Yale, "Custodian of the Keys of the Treasury" in 1701, then located at Saybrook.

OLD SILLTOWN

Again, in 1775, Lieutenant David Fithian Sill entered the Continental Army. He commanded a company of one hundred men raised in three days in Lyme, and marched to Roxbury near Boston. In 1776 he proceeded with the army in their campaign against Lord Howe, who, with the British force was located in and near New York City. A letter written by him dated from New York in August, 1776, is preserved by the author, in which he states as follows:

"I am well, though 'tis sickly here. I cannot write anything concerning affairs here, only to say that we expect an attack within three or four days at the farthest. General Howe has about fifteen thousand troops; we have a much superior number, though many are sick, however, we think there is enough to engross him."

He soon rose to the post of Lieutenant Colonel of the First Continental Line, and served in the Revolutionary War under his uncle, General Samuel Holden Parsons, also under Jedidiah Huntington. After the war Colonel Sill was frequently elected to the Legislature, and held the office of Justice of the Peace and Town Clerk for fifty years.

He was a charter member of the "Society of the Cincinnati," that depleted band of army officers of the Continental Army, which gathered on the banks of the Hudson at General Baron von Steuben's headquarters (that brave Prussian officer) in the old Verplank house at Fishkill, which is still standing and preserved by the Sons and daughters of the American Revolution, and there formed a society to promote the principles as stated below.

OLD SILLTOWN

This society, named from the distinguished Roman, Lucius Quintus Cincinnatus, adopted these principles as its basis:

First. An increased devotion to preserve inviolate the exalted rights and liberties of human nature, for which they had fought and bled.

Second. An unalterable determination to promote and cherish between the respective states union and national honor.

Third. To render permanent the cordial affection existing among the officers, to cultivate brotherly kindness and substantial acts of beneficence towards the officers and their families."

Some of the commissions of Colonel David Fithian Sill have been lost, but two are preserved; one, which was signed by Governor Fitch, of Connecticut, and was given in the 33rd year of the reign of his Majesty, King George 2nd, 1759, and was in the possession of Nettie Sill, of Oklahoma, not a lineal descendant, who lately has donated it to the Historical Society of the city of Oklahoma; the other in the possession of W. Griswold Burt, of Evanston, a great grandson, which was signed by Governor John Trumbull, of Connecticut.

His powder horn and gun, carried through the war, are preserved. John Sill, of Ashtabula, Ohio, a great grandson, who has the former, states in a letter that his father informed him before his death that it was made and given to Colonel Sill by an Indian scout and is a relic of the French War in 1759 and 1760. It has drawn on its surface maps and names of places in the eastern part of New York state and the western part of Massachusetts and Connecticut. The gun is owned by

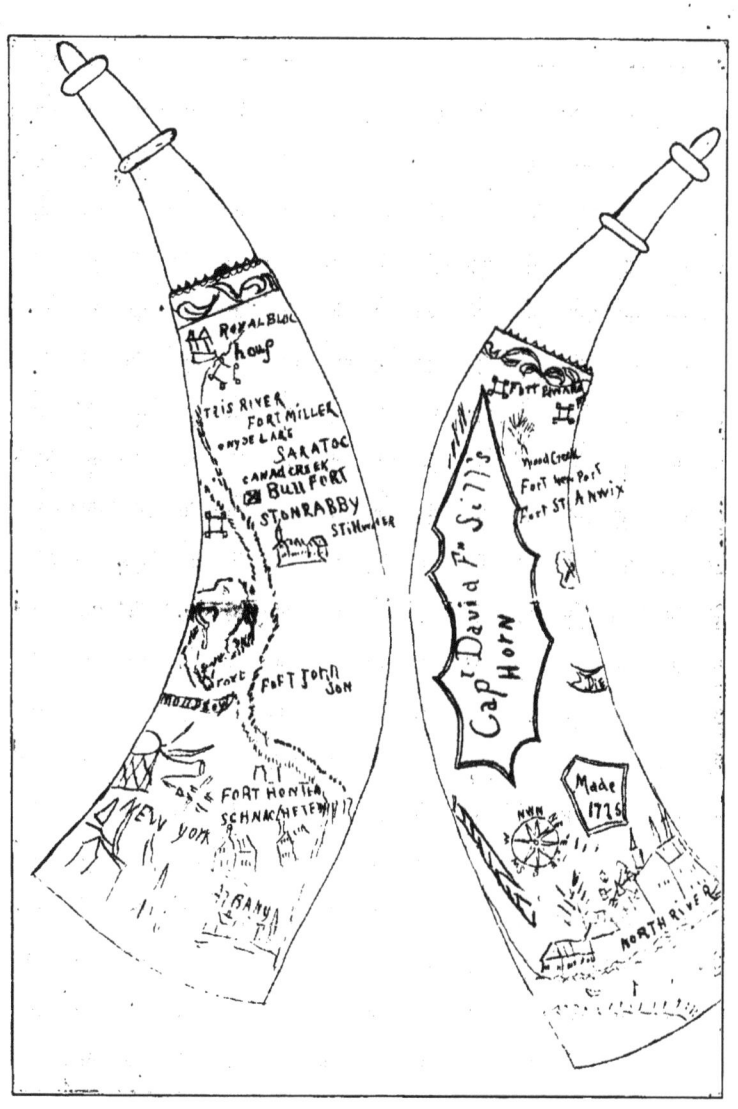

CAPT. DAVID FITHIAN SILL'S POWDER HORN.
Note—This is a Very Poor Drawing. The Carving on the Horn Itself is Wonderfully Well Done.

OLD SILLTOWN

a great grandson, W. G. Burt, Evanston, Ill. George Bodge, the historian, says this pattern of gun was called a "Snapance."

Colonel David Fithian Sill's service in connection with the war of the Revolution began at the very start of the trouble, as indicated by records in the adjutant general's office at Hartford. The following letters briefly specify of his services:

STATE OF CONNECTICUT.

Adjutant General's Office.
Hartford, Oct. 14, 1892.

Mrs. Sarah Wells Burt—
Madam:—

This may certify that the name of David F. Sill appears on the record in this office as Lieutenant in Captain Joseph Jewett's company, Lexington Alarm list, town of Lyme, served nine days.

Next appears as Captain 1st company 6th Continental Regiment. Commissioned May 1st, discharged December 10th, 1775, re-entered service in 1776.

Next appears as Captain 10th Continental Regiment, re-organized from the 6th Continental Regiment, for the year 1776.

Next appears as Lieutenant Col. 1st Regiment Conn., line, Commissioned Major January 1st, 1777. Promoted to Lieutenant-Col., commission dated March 13th, 1778—paid from March 5th—continued in '81.

OLD SILLTOWN

Next appears in Connecticut Cincinnati Society, 1783, as Lieutenant-Colonel from Lyme. Time of service, May 5th, 1778, to October, '80. No records in this office as early as 1759. These might be found in Colonial History.

Very respectfully,

WM. H. TUBBS,
Asst. Adjt. Genl.

NATIONAL SOCIETY SONS OF THE AMERICAN REVOLUTION.

Smithsonian Institution.

Washington, D. C., Sept. 27, 1892.

Dear Madam:—

Mrs. Keim has referred to me your letter of inquiry concerning service in the Revolutionary War by David Fithian Sill, of Lyme, Conn. I have examined the official record of Connecticut men in the Revolution as published by the state and find that David Fithian Sill was Lieutenant of the Lyme company called out at the time of the Lexington Alarm in April, 1775. On May 1, 1775, he was commissioned Captain of 1st Company, 6th Continental Regiment of Connecticut, under Colonel Samuel Holden Parsons, serving during siege of Boston. He was mustered out of service December 10, 1775, and re-entered in 1776 as Captain in Colonel Parsons' 10th Continental Regiment of Connecticut as re-organized; this regiment marched with Washington's command to New York and served in Battle of Long Island, etc. In January, 1777, he was commissioned Major of 1st Regiment Connecti-

OLD SILLTOWN

cut Continental Line, under Colonel Jedidiah Huntington, and promoted to Lieutenant-Colonel on March 13, 1778, serving until October, 1781. He is enrolled as a member of the Society of the Cincinnati in Connecticut.

It is probable that other detailed record of service may be obtained if you write to the Adjutant General of Connecticut at Hartford.

I hope that the above information may prove interesting to you and will gladly render further assistance in preserving the memory of such a soldier.

Very truly yours,
A. HOWARD CLARK,
Secretary-General Sons American Revolution.

Mrs. Sarah Welles Burt,
1723 Chicago, Ave.,
Evanston, Ill.

Lieutenant-Colonel David Fithian Sill died in 1813 at the age of eighty. He was extensively known throughout the state and designated Colonel Sill.

The following obituary appeared in the "Connecticut Gazette," printed in New London the week after his death. It is supposed to have been written by Judge John Griswold, of Black Hall:

"Died at Silltown, Lyme, the 9th of January, 1813, Colonel David Fithian Sill, Town Clerk, aged 80 years, an officer of the Revolutionary War. He possessed a clear head and a sound heart, was brave almost to temerity, yet prudent

OLD SILLTOWN

as brave, possessed the frankness of the officer and the suavity of the gentleman, with a mind peculiarly adapted to business. He received all the honors of office his native town could bestow, and having lived a life of usefulness to the last, was gathered to his fathers among the regrets and respect of his numerous relatives and friends."

The Colonel's wife died in 1815. Their children were: Thomas   John   David   Mary   Louis

George Griswold Sill, historian of the family, was interested in having a monument erected to the memory of this distinguished officer and ancestor. He said, "there were none in the cemetery who deserved this remembrance more than he," a brave defender of his country, yet there is but a simple tablet with inscription to mark his grave. He was not known as "David Fithian," but all over the state as "Colonel Sill."

DESCENDANTS OF JOSEPH SILL THE SECOND.

Fifth Generation
Richard Sill.

Another Revolutionary soldier was Richard Sill, fifth son of Lieutenant John, who graduated from Yale College in 1775. He entered the Continental Army as Lieutenant in 1776, was on Long Island at the time of the battle there and was with the army at King's Bridge. He spent the winter with the army at Valley Forge. In 1782 he was appointed Aide-de-camp to the American General, Lord Sterling. He was known as Major Sill and was in the American Army from 1876 to close of war. After the war he studied law with Aaron Burr and settled in the practice of that profession at Albany, N. Y. Tradition says he was one of the council to try Andre.

He was Counselor of Law for the County of Albany, and Representative of the General Assembly of New York. He married the daughter of Colonel Francis Nicol, of Bethlehem, N. Y., a worthy gentleman who adopted him as his own son.

Their sons were William Nicol Sill, who married Margaret Mather, daughter of Samuel Mather of Lyme, and John Lee Sill, who married Abigail Leverett Noyes, daughter of William Noyes, Esq., of Lyme, who built and occupied the Colonial home now owned by Miss Florence Griswold. John Lee Sill, his son-in-law, built the original of the residence on Lyme street, now owned and occupied by Joseph Huntington, Esq.

OLD SILLTOWN

Failing in health, Mr. Richard Sill had a keen desire to see some of his own family, and so sent for his father in Lyme to come and visit him. However, before the day had passed he was taken worse and died in a few hours.

His death occurred June 4th, 1790, in the 34th year of his age. There were many eulogies of him at the time of his death.

The following notice is from the Albany Gazette of June 7th, 1790:

"On Friday afternoon at three o'clock departed this life at Bethlehem, the seat of Col. Francis Nicol, in the 34th year of his age, Richard Sill, Esq., counselor at law and Representative to the general assembly of this state for the County of Albany, and yesterday his remains were interred in the family burying ground at that place, attended by a number of his connections and friends from this city. It would be a piece of injustice not to observe on this occasion that, independent of the services of this gentleman in the army of the United States during the late war, his good sense, affable manner and amiable disposition, added to the strictest integrity in public as well as private life, render his character in the highest degree respectable and his death a public misfortune as well as a most distressing loss."

Richard Sill's descendants intermarried with the early families of Albany, N. Y.; Van Renslers, Ludlows, Russels and Livingstons.

In 1854 Mr. Geo. G. Sill wrote as follows:

OLD SILLTOWN

"In 1804 his sons, William Nicol Sill and John Lee Sill, of Albany, came to Silltown to hunt up their cousins, and were highly pleased with their visit. At that time their father's three brothers and two sisters were living and everybody seemed glad to see them for their father's sake, as he was one of the few men of whom it might be said "he was universally beloved."

A descendant of Richard Sill, of the American Revolution, through his son, William Nicol Sill, is Mr. Howard Sill, a prominent architect of Baltimore, Md. He is eligible in eighteen different lines, and is an active member of the Society of Colonial Wars. He has collected much historical data concerning the achievements of his Colonial ancestors.

OLD SILLTOWN

John Sill, the Third.

John Sill, the 3rd (who was son of Lieutenant John, the 2nd), was the ancestor (through his son, Henry Sill), of Lieutenant-Governor George Griswold Sill, of Hartford, Conn. He (John Sill, the 3d), married Elizabeth Griswold, daughter of Mr. George Griswold, sister of George and Nathaniel Griswold, of New York City. For an account of the above mentioned Lieutenant-Governor George Griswold Sill see 7th generation.

OLD SILLTOWN

Silas Sill and His Sons.

Silas Sill, fourth son of Lieutenant John, built his home on Sill lands near the entrance to Hamburg Road. His wife was Hannah Griswold, of Giant's Neck, daughter of Rev. George Griswold and sister of George and Nathaniel Gris-

SILAS SILL'S HOME, BUILT IN 1786.

wold, successful merchants in New York City in the line of ship chandlery.

His three sons were: Richard, George and Horace. Richard removed to Albany and became a successful merchant. He died young at the age of 29 years. It is recorded of him that his strict attention to business, his exemplary moral deportment obtained for him the esteem of all his acquaintances, and there was none that knew him but greatly lamented his loss.

OLD SILLTOWN

George Sill, Second Son of Silas Sill,

Of Silltown, became a clergyman of the Dutch Reformed church. A genealogy and history of the Sill family, which he compiled was, after his death, published by his daughter in 1859, Mrs. Louise Sill Betts, now of Denver, Colo. The author is indebted to this genealogy for much guidance in securing incidents related in this book.

It is recorded that "Mr. George S. Sill was a man of large frame and vigorous constitution, genial temperament and a heart empty of selfishness, full of warm sympathy and good

HOME OF HORACE SILL IN 1858.

will towards all mankind. He seemed more desirous of 'growing heavenward' than of growing rich, and has doubtless found his recompense better than gold or silver. He was remarkable for his power of memory. His last end was peace."

He died at the home of Mr. Horace Sill (his brother), Lyme, Conn., May 20th, 1859, aged 58 years, and interment was in the Lyme cemetery.

Horace Sill, Third Son of Silas Sill.

Horace Sill, 3rd son of Silas Sill, engaged in business in New York with his uncles, George and Nathaniel Griswold, in 1853. In 1858 he removed to Lyme, purchasing Mr. John Hart's homestead, where he remained till his death. The death of an only son, Richard Griswold Sill, aged 10 years, in 1853, who was drowned in the Connecticut River, was a serious blow to both him and Mrs. Sill, from which they never recovered. Mrs. Sill survived the death of her husband several years.

OLD SILLTOWN

DESCENDANTS OF JOSEPH SILL, THE SECOND.

Sixth Generation

1st Generation	2nd Generation	3rd Generation	4th Generation	5th Generation	6th Generation
John Sill of England	Joseph Sill the First	Joseph Sill the Second	Lieutenant John Sill	David Fithian Sill and Sarah Griswold	Sons: Thomas John David Daughters: Mary Louise

Two sons of David Fithian Sill died young—David in infancy, John by drowning. His two daughters married Matsons, Louise married David Matson and Mary married Deacon Nathanial Matson. This latter union was strongly opposed by their parents; for what reason is not known. But Nathanial and Mary were obdurate. The deacon placed a ladder at the window and Mary availed herself of this means of escape and they were married.

Her high ruffed cap, the fashion of those days, and beautiful gown of the style now known as empire, ornamented with a tasteful ribbon bow at the waist, was most becoming, enhancing the beauty of her bright, youthful countenance, as is evidenced in her portrait still preserved by a grand-nephew, George Sill Welles, of Park Ridge, Ill.

MARY (POLLY) SILL

OLD SILLTOWN

Thomas Sill.

Thomas Sill was the only surviving child of Colonel David Fithian Sill. He inherited his father's estate and purchased lands of the other Sills as they removed to other towns and states. He was born in 1769, erected his commodious dwelling on inherited land near where his father's stood, situ-

HOME OF CAPT. THOMAS SILL, BUILT IN 1799—WINTER VIEW.

ated at a slight bend in the road leading up the hill in Silltown. This Colonial mansion, now more than a hundred years old, is still standing and in a good state of preservation. It is said to have been built by ship carpenters. The floors of this house are of solid oak planks, short in length; the outer doors divided, built after the Dutch style of architecture; the lintels grooved in the columns and otherwise ornamented in fret work. The tall, stately elms, maples, horsechestnuts and catalpa trees adorning the lawn, have now grown to such enormous size and their branches so wide-spreading that driving up the main road in summer one scarcely discerns the stately old colonial mansion.

Into this attractive home Captain Sill took his bride in 1799. She was the daughter of Samuel Mather, of Lyme, and was the namesake of her aunt, Mehitable Mather, her father's sister, who married that distinguished Revolutionary officer of the First Continental Line, Major-General Samuel Holden Parsons, whom the family records state, lost his life when visiting the Connecticut Western Reserve Lands in Ohio, where he was accidentally drowned in the Big Beaver River, and was buried on its banks near its confluence with the Ohio. It is not known if his grave is marked with even a tablet or inscription, much less a monument suitable to his rank as an officer. Investigation does not discover his last resting place. In the family lot at Middleton, Ohio, is erected a monument to his memory with inscription of his service to his country.

Mrs. Sill was a grand-daughter of Deacon Thomas Griswold, son of Judge John, a descendant of the first Matthew Griswold, who married Anna Wolcott. She was, through her father, a descendant of Rev. Richard Mather, of Dorchester, Mass., who came (history says) to this country on the ship "Angel Gabriel," from Toxeth Park, England, to escape religious persecution.

OLD SILLTOWN

Mrs. Sill's father, Samuel Mather, had become wealthy through his trade with the West Indies, exchanging home products for the products of the Islands. Her wedding dowry of $30,000 was a fortune in those days. Her trousseau was elaborate and costly. It included rich silk gowns with high healed slippers to match, high back-combs, beaded bags, fans and many accessories of dress. Some of these were preserved by her daughters, Misses Nancy and Mary Sill, even to the advent of her grandchildren who, when visiting the homestead, were interested in studying their style and listening to tales of this dear grandmother long since passed away.

She left her young and numerous family at the age of forty-one years. These young housekeepers, not knowing the value of old documents, laid away in the attic for preserva-

SAMUEL MATHER HOMESTEAD, OLD LYME.

tion, destroyed deeds and grants of lands, given by the Nahantic and Pequoit Indians, the original occupants of this region, which would be highly valued at the present time.

Old household effects and jewels, preserved by the loving

OLD SILLTOWN

aunts and handed down through generations, proved the descendants' connection with early ancestors four generations and more back, establishing eligibility to membership in the Societies of the Colonial Sires and Dames of America, should they so desire.

The author remembers seeing the old Franklin stoves stored in the barn of her grandfather, that were in use long before her time in her grandfather's home. There were large and small pewter platters, which must have been in possession of our ancestors brought from foreign lands; the old Dutch clock is still preserved by a great-granddaughter; there were also high-post bedsteads, now so much valued, high boys, which were later converted into modern bureaus and dressers. There were also tusters for high-post bedsteads in the attic used by our grandmother, Mrs. Thomas Sill. There were draped hangings of English cretonne cloths in varied colorings, with landscapes and beautiful birds in decoration. In the upper hallway of Captain Sill's home was a portrait of a colored boy painted on wood. A grandson of Captain Thomas Sill tells the author his Aunt Mary (Mrs. Mary Sill, daughter of Captain Thomas) said this was a likeness of a slave boy named Daniel, a descendant of a slave owned by Lieutenant John (Fourth Generation), who had been owned and brought up by the family. He was drowned in an attempt to save one of the younger members of the Sill family who fell overboard from a scow in the river, which was bringing hay from the salt meadows. This portrait was painted by William Banning, of Laysville.

Captain Thomas Sill was a genial companion, generous hearted, a man of strict integrity. He inherited the patriotism

OLD SILLTOWN

of his father, Colonel David Fithian Sill; was Captain in the State Militia. It was in the spacious front upper chamber of his home that he entertained his company of one hundred men when they met for consultation in the interests of this organization. The floor of this apartment has ever since been sunken from their weight.

HOME OF THOMAS SILL.
View From Farm Yard.

The following pictures were taken after alteration of the home. The Colonial entrance has been lost by the large porch addition—rear buildings have been torn down.

OLD SILLTOWN

Captain Thomas Sill was a Mason. His Masonic apron is still preserved by a great-grandson, William Griswold Burt, of Chicago and Evanston, Ill.

He led principally an agricultural life, cultivating his farm in Silltown and in Black Hall. Both Mr. and Mrs. Sill were owners in the Connecticut Western Reserve Lands, a tract 100 miles in width. This he visited on horseback before railroads were in existence. A letter written by Mr. Thomas Sill from Warren, Ohio, in 1821, to his wife at the

HOME OF CAPT. THOMAS SILL.
View From Main Street.

time of his trip to his Western Reserve Lands is now in the possession of William Griswold Burt. In this letter he speaks of the difficulty of realizing any money on the sale of any of these lands.

In a late memorial of William C. Young, of New York City, a civil engineer, one of the early surveyors and promoters of railroads in this country, who also developed plans with others for the Groton Water Works of that city, is an account of the Connecticut Reserve Lands, which I quote. He purchased five thousand acres himself, and laid the foundations of the city now named after him, "Youngstown."

CONNECTICUT WESTERN RESERVE LANDS.

"A proper understanding of this strange mingling of Connecticut and Ohio involves a bit of Colonial history which is very interesting and but little known. In 1662 King Charles II granted a charter to the Connecticut Colony. The limits of this colony were to be bounded by Massachusetts on the north, Long Island Sound on the south, Narragansett River on the east, and the Pacific Ocean on the west; virtually a strip of territory less than 100 miles wide, running like a narrow ribbon right across the continent. It is amusing to lay this bit of ancient history upon a modern map and find Chicago within the Connecticut limits, Salt Lake swallowed, until crossing the Sierra Nevadas and California the Pacific boundary is reached. There was a long controversy in relation to this claim, which was finally settled by the assigning by Connecticut to the United States of all lands west of Pennsylvania, reserving only a tract 120 miles long and a mean of 50 miles wide between Lake Erie and the 41st parallel of latitude. This tract was known as the "Connecticut Western Reserve."

Mrs. Thomas Sill, whose maiden name was Mahitable Mather, daughter of Samuel Mather, of Lyme, was also descended, through her father, from Major General Humphrey Atherton, of the Continental Army of 1665, whose daughter, Catherine Atherton, married the son of Rev. Richard Mather

MASONIC APRON OWNED BY CAPT. THOMAS SILL.
A Reduced Copy. Original is in Bright Colors—Gold and Silver on Fine Sheep Skin.

OLD SILLTOWN

and removed to Lyme, they being some of the first settlers. Major-General Humphrey Atherton, whose accidental death occurred when reviewing his troops on Boston Common, was noted for his bravery. Shurtcliff's history of Boston says of him, "He was a man of considerable importance in the colony, having held important offices and at the time of his death being an incumbent of the highest military position in Massachusetts. Orcult's History of Dorchester says of him:

"He was energetic and firm in character. As an incident illustrating his great courage and presence of mind, he was sent to Percassuss, an Indian Sachem, with twenty men to demand three hundred fathoms of wampum. Percassuss refused to allow him to come into his presence. Finally Atherton led his men to the wigwam of Percassuss and entered himself, pistol in hand, seized Percassuss by the hair and dragged him out, threatening to kill the first man who interfered. He may be said to have died in the service of his country for, returning home on September 16th, 1661, from Boston Common, where he had been reviewing his troups, he was thrown from his horse and killed instantly."

He was buried with great pomp and ceremony. His epitaph is carefully cut upon the marble tablet resting on the sarcophagus in which his body is entombed, under the image of a naked sword, an emblem of the highest honor. The following epitaph is placed upon his tablet:

OLD SILLTOWN

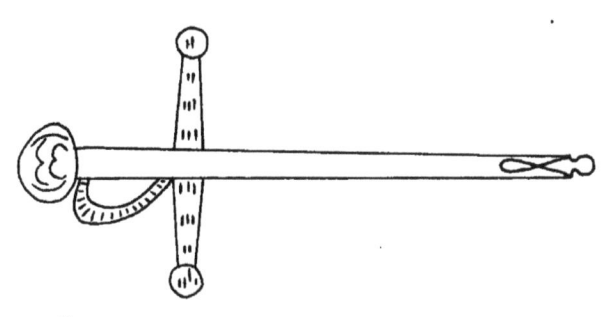

"MAJOR-GENERAL HUMPHREY ATHERTON.

"Here lyes our Captaine and Major of Suffolk was withall
A Godly magistrate was he and Major-General
Two troups of hors with hime here came
    Such worth his love did crave.
Ten companyes of foot also movering
    Marched to his grave.
Let all that read be sure to keep the faith as he hath done.
With Christ he lives, now crowned his name
    was Humphrey Atherton.
        He dyed the 16th of September, 1661."

Thomas Sill died in 1852. His children were Phoebe, John, Margaret, Nancy, Henry, Sarah, Mary, and Francis.

In 1853 Mr. Oliver Lay and Mr. Israel Matson, who had been appointed as distributors of Mr. Thomas Sill's estate, drew off and retained copies of Mr. Thomas Sill's will, of the inventory of his estate, of the administration account as proved and allowed, of the expense account of H. M. Waite for expenses made in settling the estate and a copy of the record of distribution of the estate as made by the distributors. These

OLD SILLTOWN

copies, by reason of the kindness of Mr. Daniel Lay, of Layesville, are now in the possession of Mr. W. Griswold Burt, of Evanston and Chicago, Ill. It is interesting to note the care, the neatness and the exactness with which these papers were prepared.

The western boundary of the old Sill farm, operated by Captain Thomas Sill, was the Lieutenant River, which was

VIEW OF LIEUTENANT RIVER AT THE SILL LANDINGS.

at that time navigable at high tide as far up as his farm by small vessels. There were three landings on Captain Sill's shores, known as the Board Landing, the Hay Landing and the Log Landing. An old resident of Lyme, the late Captain John Lester, stated in 1907 that he remembered when these vessels were built across the river from Mr. Sill's farm, for use in the Coast Trading in which the Sills were owners, and his

OLD SILLTOWN

father had stated that the Connecticut River shad were caught as far up Lieutenant River as Log Landing, and that a fishhouse was once situated there.

George Griswold Sill states, in a letter to one of his cousins, that immense logs were floated down the Connecticut River from New Hampshire and Vermont and up the Lieutenant River to the Log Landing and from there conveyed

VIEW OF LIEUTENANT RIVER AT THE SILL LANDINGS.

overland to the saw mills located farther north, where Laysville now stands. They were there converted into building material and brought back to Board Landing and from there shipped to Long Island and other points along the Sound. He also tells of a grove (which has long since been cut down) on a knoll overlooking the river, then called Harmony Grove, where the family held their reunions and 4th of July celebra-

OLD SILLTOWN

tions in which he, as a boy, participated. Frequently Indian arrow heads have been turned up when plowing, thus indicating that Indians traversed this land.

The long range of high hills, covered with dense forests, which border the Lieutenant River on its western shore, are also recorded in the town records of Hamburg as having been Captain Thomas Sill's possessions. Their reflections in the waters of the river form an attractive back-ground for this secluded spot. Now, as then, the eagles and fish-hawks here have their eyries in the tall treetops and hover over the river watching for their prey, seizing it in their talons and bearing it away, even as they did in the days of old Silltown. A few years ago a descendant of Captain Sill shot one of these huge birds which measured within two inches of six feet from tip to tip. In recent years these hills on the western shores of Lieutenant River have been in the possession of Wm. Coult, and are now generally spoken of as the "Billy Coult Hills," but they are now mostly owned by Mr. Robert Hall. Mr. George Griswold Sill, in a letter to Mrs. Mary Sill, has said, "But ancient Silltown is an interesting place when we go back in imagination and look at the people who lived in those early days. Many are the changes that have taken place since those days, but no changes can deprive old Silltown of its history."

DESCENDANTS OF JOSEPH SILL, THE SECOND.

Seventh Generation

John Sill, son of Thomas Sill, left descendants. His oldest son and namesake, John Sill, served in the Civil War in America and resided on a portion of the Western Reserve Lands in Ashtabula, Ohio.

Henry Sill, son of Thomas Sill, died at the age of 22 years, is recorded as having been a talented young man. He gave promises of a brilliant future and was a student and an able writer. He was a great favorite with his sisters Mary and Nancy. Mary Sill always believed that he was not actually dead at the time he was buried, that he was in a deep stupor and that he was in reality actually buried alive. Mary Sill's belief in this could never be dislodged. His last illness was yellow fever, for which he was given the then customary treatment of severe bleeding.

Miss Nancy Sill, fourth child of Captain Thomas Sill, was possessed of a quiet, retiring, modest nature, who was exceptionally gracious and always devoted to the poor, who ever found in her their benefactor. She was a devoted disciple of her Divine Master. She died in 1852; she had never been married and lived, in company with her sister, Miss Mary Sill, in the old family homestead of her father.

OLD SILLTOWN

Mary Sill.

As above stated, Mary Sill had lived in the old house erected by Mr. Thomas Sill, with her sister, Nancy Sill, and after her sister's death, for many years she lived here alone with an attendant, during which time she superintended the management of her properties. She married Mr. Schadrach Sill, of Grassy Hill, a distant connection and descendant of the Thomas Sill (fourth generation) branch of the family. An old letter states, "On the occasion of her wedding she was attended by a few intimate friends and her pastor, Mr. and Mrs. Brainard. A small reception was held at her home, where she received the congratulations of her friends." Mr. Sill lived only four years, and again Mary Sill was left alone in the old home of her father. Here she lived with her servant to the ripe old age of ninety-one years, surviving all her brothers and sisters. The beautiful tribute to her, published in the Lyme paper by Bishop Sabine, of New York and Lyme, so perfectly described her that we quote it here below:

> "Mrs. Mary Sill, whose death we chronicled in our last issue, was a life-long resident of this town.
>
> "It is an interesting fact she was born, lived and died in the same dwelling which had been owned and occupied by her father and with which we are so familiar. There are very few persons of whom it can be said in our country, with its constantly increasing and rapidly changing population that for nearly a century they found a home in one house.
>
> "Mrs. Sill, being born in 1812, was upwards of 91 at the time of her death. She was a daughter of Captain Thomas Sill and a descendant of the noted Mather family. She was religiously brought up and the results of early training were apparent through her use-

ful life. She united with the Congregational Church here at an early age, in which she retained her membership until the last.

"We may not close this notice of a long and well-spent life without a word of its kindness and Christian character. Mrs. Sill was no half-hearted servant of her Divine Master. She was generously concerned for the welfare of those about her. Many acts of kindness testified to this concern. As to her faith in God, in Christ, in her Bible, in prayer, it was clear, simple, firm, strong, and thus was the source of much that was good and beautiful in her attractive

MARY SILL.

character. Her smile was a benediction and her sweet and kindly face will not soon be forgotten by those who had come to know and love her.

"She was most decided in her Christian character and zeal. So has passed to her eternal reward and rest one for whose life and example our town may be grateful and whose memory should be long cherished among us with loving respect."

OLD SILLTOWN

The following is taken from "In Memoriam" of Mary Sill, published by Sarah Sill Welles Burt:

"Mary Sill was educated at Mrs. Phoebe Noyes' private home school at Norwich and the Kellogg Seminary, N. Y. Her mother dying in 1831 and her brother John moving to Ohio, and sisters Phoebe and Margaret married to Mr. Chas. and Mr. John Hart of Saybrook, and Sarah to A. D. Welles, of New York City. The two sisters, Nancy and Mary, occupied the homestead with their father, who died in 1852. Miss Nancy Sill died in 1862. Miss Mary Sill then married Mr. Shadrack Sill, of Grassy Hill, who lived but four years.

"During her entire life Mrs. Sill resided in the old home of her father.

"Mrs. Sill had a bright and active mind, with high and noble aims. She was public-spirited, interested in events occurring in the world, was decided in her opinions, was of a deeply religious nature and early in life united with the church of her fathers (the Congregational). She was, during all her life, devoted to missions, and gave in her youth her simple girlish jewels for the cause, and could never be persuaded to accept a gift of that nature in after life.

"The companionship of relatives and friends was a great pleasure to her; she was always hospitable and entertaining in conversation. Letters (of which she received many were her solace, and she continued to write those she loved best almost to the very last.

"She was of a cheerful and happy disposition and patient under every trial. Several periods of illness were borne with a patience which never failed. The last illness from a fall and broken limb, was painful in the extreme. When suffering thus she said, 'Let me go! Let me go!' Thanking the loved ones bending over her, and kissing them, she bade each one good-bye gently, waving her hands, saying she hoped to meet them in a Better Land. It was not long ere the Lord took her to himself. Her noble countenance, calm in death, wearing almost a smile, bespoke the peace of the soul released from its earthly fetters to join the company of the redeemed in Heaven.

OLD SILLTOWN

"Services were held at her home, Rev. Chas. Villiers, her pastor, officiating; speaking appreciative words with reading of scripture and singing of her favorite hymns, 'Jesus, Lover of My Soul,' 'Nearer, My God, to Thee.'

"The casket, draped with flowers in lavish abundance, expressing the love of many friends, was borne to the cemetery by her grand-nephews and friends, Messrs. William and John Peckham and Mr. Richard Hart of New York; Prof. Bartlett, Mr. Thomas Farwell, Mr. Charles Sill. Dr. Villiers then repeated the burial services when our revered, aged and honored friend and citizen was laid to rest in 'The Sill Enclosure,' amid the ancestors of seven generations."

TRIBUTE BY CAROLINE ANN MATSON TERRY.

We all (myself and sons) loved Mrs. Sill and I dare not think what Lyme will be without her and my beloved brother. I already begin to dread a visit there. Mrs. Sill seemed well when I saw her last summer; I little thought I was bidding her good-bye for the last time.

She was always thinking and planning some way of doing good to others. I remember so well when but a child, hearing her with a neighbor contrive ways to help the needy and destitute at home and abroad, and denying themselves that they might give to missions. They have "entered into rest" and heard the glad welcome, "Good and faithful servants," but the results of their labors still go on.

TRIBUTE BY A GRAND NEPHEW AT THE TIME OF HER DEATH.

Dear Aunt Mary is laid away; "her day is gone, her deeds are done." It makes me feel very sad that I shall never see her more. How many grand and pleasant things we can remember of her. Her life on this earth was one well lived. She "so lived that when her summons came to join the innumerable caravan that moves to that mysterious Realm" she could gladly, cheerfully sing:

> "Just as I am, without one plea,
> But that Thy blood was shed for me,
> And that Thou bid'st me come to Thee;
> O Lamb of God, I come, I come."

Women of her stamp are very few in this day and generation. Such an example of hardihood, strength, fortitude, Christian spirit is monumental. She never faltered at any obstacle that beset her walk in life because of her confidence in the guiding hand of Him whose angels had charge over her to keep her in all her ways.

Aunt Mary dwelt in the "secret places of the Most High" and "abode under the shadow of the Almighty." Death had no sting nor the grave any victory over her, still we must not weep for her. We would not, if we could, call her back into this world. Let us take pleasure in the thought that she is through with earthly cares and has reached her heavenly home beyond the skies.

NOTE.—As the final compilation of this volume was being made (November, 1912) word comes of the passing away of Caroline Ann Matson Terry, aged 91 years. During the summer just closed the writer had the pleasure of seeing this dear old lady with her same characteristic smile which he can vividly remember seeing so often during the time of his boyhood when visiting her in company with his mother Sarah Sill Welles Burt and Mrs. Mary Sill. For the notice of the death of Mrs. Terry see final chapter in this book.

OLD SILLTOWN

RESOLUTIONS.

The members of the Leucretia Shaw Chapter, of New London, Conn., "Daughters of the American Revolution," passed the following resolutions at their last meeting:

WHEREAS, God in His wisdom has taken Mrs. Mary Sill, a charter member, at an age which she attained by reason of strength and which we reverence,

RESOLVED, That we pay a tribute to that patriotism that prompted her to enroll, in 1892, her name on our honored list and that we remember with sympathy the surviving relatives.

RESOLVED, That these resolutions be entered upon the minutes of the Chapter and that a copy be sent to her friends.

MARY COOK COMSTALK, *Historian.*

Mrs. Mary Sill was greatly beloved and admired by her many nephews and nieces, many of whom are now living who can tell of the weeks and months spent with her during their summer vacations. Memory of her keen understanding of their youthful pains and pleasures with her trite words of wisdom will always remain.

On her headstone in the Lyme cemetery is inscribed the following verse of Scripture truly appropriate to her:

"She openeth her mouth with wisdom and on her tongue is the law of kindness." Prov. 31:26.

Mrs. Mary Sill, on her mother's side, was descended from

OLD SILLTOWN

Governor Francis Willouby, whose wife, Margaret Locke Taylor, was second cousin to Queen Elizabeth of England, as follows:

Mary Sill, daughter of Thomas Sill, son of David Fithian Sill and Sarah Griswold, daughter of Deacon Thomas Griswold of Black Hall, whose wife was daughter of Judge Nathanial Lynn and Susanna Willouby of Saybrook, (?) sister of Governor Francis Willouby.

Governor Willouby was the owner of large interests in Boston Harbor; his shipyards were where the Fitchburgh freight station now stands and his wharves were upon both sides of the Ferry. He was Deputy General of Massachusetts from 1665 to 1671. The Reverend Simon Bradstreet of New York, says:

"Governor Willouby desired to be buried one foot deep and to have 'ye top of grave plain, only covered with ye tops of ye grass.'"

The location of his grave is not accurately known and it is presumed that this is owing to a request of his that his grave should be left unmarked.

From the Memorial History of Boston, volume 1, page 520, we quote the following advice:

"When, in 1670, Deputy General Francis Willouby died and was buried, we were told that there were eleven full companies in attendance and that with the doleful noise of trumpet and drum in their mourning posture, three thundering volleys of shot were discharged, answered by the loud roaring of the great guns rendering the heavens with their noise at the loss of so great a man."

OLD SILLTOWN

Below is shown a picture of an old relic formerly belonging to the Willouby family and now preserved by one of their descendants. It is claimed that this relic was presented to her second cousin, Margaret Willouby, by Queen Elizabeth, together with some items contained in it (including a tablecloth embroidered by the princess during her imprisonment in

ELIZABETHIAN CHEST.

the Tower) as a mark of appreciation of her loyalty as shown by her having shared with the queen her captivity in the tower of London. It will be remembered that the imprisonment of Queen Elizabeth in the tower of London occurred before she became queen, brought about through the influence of King Philip of Spain in order to prevent her becoming queen. It is said of Queen Elizabeth that before entering the tower as she landed at the gate, she called on the soldiers to bear witness that "I come as no traitor." She flung herself on the stones in the rain and refused to enter the palace, and said "Better sitting here than in a worse place." It was finally definitely recognized that she was not an accomplice to the conspiracy for which she had been accused and was later set free.

The chest is a massive affair, seven feet in length, two feet seven inches in width and two feet seven inches high. It is made of a peculiar hard wood, originally very light in color, but darkened exceedingly by age. The quaint old carvings on the front and on the inside of the cover, the handwrought massive iron hinges and handles, the cumbersome lock and huge keys, are eloquent testimony of its age. The carvings on the outside, which are nearly worn off, evidently represent horsemen riding through a forest. At either end of the three front panels is a gallant of the Elizabethan period, long-haired, plume-hatted and a mass of ruffs and laces from neck to knees. The carvings on the inner side of the lid represent two scenes, one of Sir Walter Raleigh spreading his cloak before Queen Elizabeth; the other of a gay pleasure party in boats among small islands, with a turreted castle in the background. Between the two scenes is a coat of arms. The shield has either a crest or lines to make four quarterings.

The tradition that this chest, with the tablecloth embroidered in the tower and other valuable gifts, was given by Queen Elizabeth to Lady Margaret Willouby is claimed to be sufficiently well authenticated as to be beyond dispute.

The Raymonds, Lyndes, Griswolds and Sills of New England, trace their ancestry back to Colonel William Wil-

OLD SILLTOWN

louby, who was commissioner of the British Navy from 1648 to 1651, when he died. His son, Francis Willouby, came to New England in 1638 and returned to England in 1651. In 1652 he was appointed successor of his father as commissioner of the navy and in 1658 he was chosen member of parliament for Portsmouth. In 1662 he returned to New England and became Deputy Governor for the Massachusetts Colony in 1665, continuing in office until he died in 1675.

The great chest which had come into the Raymond family by reason of marriage with the Willoubys was brought from Block Island to New London in 1704 by Mrs. Mercy Raymond, widow of Joshua, who was a grandson of Richard, it was then known as the "Great Willouby Chest" and as the "Elizabethan Chest." From generation to generation it was handed down, it finally was bequeathed to Theodore Raymond of Springfield, Mass., the present owner, by his grandfather, Theodore Raymond of Norwich, Conn.

OLD SILLTOWN

Lieutenant Governor George Griswold Sill.

George Griswold Sill, fourth son of Henry Sill of Windsor, Conn., who was the son of Lieutenant John Sill, who was the son of Joseph Sill, the Second, son of Joseph Sill, the First, son of John Sill of England.

George Griswold Sill was born Oct. 26th, 1829. He settled in Hartford as an attorney-at-law and resided there until his death in 1907 after a long illness. He was prominent for many years and distinguished as a lawyer and statesman and held a high public office.

He was prepared for college by private tuition, graduated at Yale, A. B., 1852, attended lectures for a year at Yale Law School and afterwards became a student in the law office of the late Governor Richard D. Hubbard at Hartford. Admitted to the bar in 1854. For thirty-six years was Justice of the Peace, for many years was prosecuting grand juror and a side judge of Hartford city court. 1871-73 was recorder or judge of the same court, served three years in Hartford common council, part of the time as alderman. Elected lieutenant-governor in 1873, ticket headed by C. R. Ingersoll; re-elected 1874-75-76.

It has been said that it was difficult to find a lawyer who would take a case in opposition to him. He was Lieutenant-Governor of Connecticut and United States District Attorney under President Cleveland's administration. There were many eulogies of him after his death, one of which I quote here:

George G. Sill

JUDGE BARBOUR'S TRIBUTE TO THE MEMORY OF GEORGE G. SILL.

"It was my privilege to know Lieutenant Governor George G. Sill fifty-two years. Will you kindly give me space for a brief, humble tribute to his memory. The year he began the practice of law, I began the study of it. I well remember how awe-inspiring to a young person was his majestic presence and manner; how terrifying to such a person was his blunt speech, his sober, stern countenance, but acquaintance with him proved that beneath that austere exterior was a kind heart. My intercourse with him the last ten years has been close and intimate, having had an office on the same floor with him, and until a few months ago, when he became confined to his home, I saw and talked with him most every day.

"There is sincere mourning today among the lawyers and others occupying the floor, for like the Israelite 'in him was no guile,' and to know him thoroughly was to esteem him highly. His infirmities of late have prevented his carrying on the extensive practice he had for years. His faltering step about the street and his marked appearance of physical feebleness have excited the commiseration of his acquaintances. There is probably no man at the bar who has the respect and confidence of his brethren and the community to a greater extent than he. There survives but one lawyer who was a resident in Hartford when he came to the bar, the Hon. Charles E. Perkins. May the day be distant when obituary words shall be spoken of him.

"Mr. Sill was a very impressive public speaker. I recall a very striking illustration of this on the occasion of the meeting of the bar to take notice of the death of Governor Richard D. Hubbard, his former instructor. I think I hazard nothing in saying that in tender affection for the subject of his remarks, in eloquent just eulogy, and classical finish of language, his address was a gem not surpassed by that of any of the distinguished speakers on that occasion. I recall how touching were his closing words, "His halting faith no longer darkens his existence. What he longed so much to believe and know he has realized in that unknown and mysterious future which lies beyond the confines of this mortal life." These grand words carry the implication that his own faith was in no wise weak. Until he became too feeble to attend church his hearty participations in the beautiful Episcopal service at his church home (Trinity Church) showed him to be a humble worshipper of the Unseen One, and a believer in immortality.

"Mr. Sill had sore family trials, prominent among which was the accident to his beloved namesake, a son whose immediate escape from death seemed miraculous. The death of that son after a few years of professional association with his father was a blow from which the father never recovered and he aged more rapidly after that shock, etc., etc., etc."

When Governor of the State he was presented with a set of silverware by the Connecticut Senate in 1868. Concerning the long disappearance of this silver, I quote the following from a recent article in the press:

FOUND AFTER MANY YEARS.
SON OF LIEUTENANT GOVERNOR SILL RECEIVES SILVER SET, STOLEN YEARS AGO.

After being held in a pawn shop for 31 years a set of silverware stolen from the house of Lieutenant Governor Sill of Connecticut, was recovered last week by the police of Hartford and turned over to William Raymond Sill of New York, a son of the governor.

In 1877, burglars stole several thousand dollars' worth of silverware and jewelry from Governor Sill's house, including a highly prized set of silver presented by the Connecticut

OLD SILLTOWN

Senate in 1868. Governor Sill offered a reward at the time and the police, according to the old Hartford records, spent much time on the case.

The silver service is in almost perfect condition. The chest, made of leather and carrying the coat of arms of Connecticut, was slightly cut. Each piece of silver bears the date of 1867 and the inscription of Lieutenant Governor Sill

The son of Lieutenant Governor Sill referred to by Judge Barbour was:

GEORGE ELIOT SILL.

Born in Hartford, 1862, struck down in the midst of his career at the early age of about forty years. He graduated from the West Middle School in his native city and was a freshman at the Hartford High School when he was seriously injured in a railroad accident at Stony Creek during the summer of 1877, in which both of his feet were severed. Everything known to medical science was done to restore him to comparative normal condition but the infirmity always preyed deeply on his mind and produced in him a very retiring disposition. He entered high school a year or so later and graduated in 1882. He matriculated at Amherst and in 1886 received a Degree of Bachelor of Science. He studied law with his father, then Lieutenant Governor and was admitted to the Hartford County bar in 1888. His general ability, especially in law, made him always in demand. Mentally, he was very active and received many honors. He was delegate to many conventions. The position of Collector of Customs was offered him through Congressman Sperry of that State, but he declined, preferring to practice law with his father who needed him in conducting the large law practice of his office.

His last case was before the Court of Common Appeals where he appeared on the morning of the day in which he was taken ill and died after an illness of ten weeks' duration.

He was a member of many patriotic societies—The Reform of New York, The Press Club, The Society of Colonial Wars, Sons of American Revolutions.

OLD SILLTOWN

Silltown Chapel

On the side of the road running by the Sill farm lands about three hundred yards from Thomas Sill's homestead there stands the old district school house. It has many times been repaired yet has not lost its original design. There the children of the neighborhood received their education. Among

SILLTOWN CHAPEL.

the teachers of those early days, my own aunt, Mrs. Mary Sill, has stated there were such instructors as the late Governor Buckingham, then a young man, who rose to distinction in later life. It was customary in those days that the teacher be taken into the home and cared for, given room and lodging by the various residents of the district in turn.

OLD SILLTOWN

This school house, ten or more years ago, was repaired by Mrs. Mary Sill and the other residents of the neighborhood and was converted into a chapel where religious services and social gatherings of the people of the neighborhood have since been held. The building is no longer used as a school house, the district schools having all been consolidated with those of the town and removed to a central building in the town of Lyme. At the present writing (1912) this old Silltown Chapel is in fairly good repair, and it is the expectation of the residents of the locality to use it for prayer meetings on Sunday afternoons during the coming fall and winter. It is also serving a good purpose as a place of meeting of the new organization of Boy Scouts which has recently been formed in the neighborhood.

LOCATION OF THE HOMES OF THE SILL FAMILIES.

The house of Captain John Sill was situated about where the present home of Mr. Daniel Davidson now stands. John Sill left this house to his only son, Joseph Sill, the 1st, who in turn left this house to his son Joseph Sill, the 2nd, who resided there thirty years and removed to North Lyme. Joseph Sill, the 2nd, in turn left this house to his oldest son, Lieutenant John Sill, the 2nd.

John Sill, the 3d, second son of Lieutenant John Sill, the 2nd, built his house across the street from his father's and next to his was built the home of Silas Sill, which house is now standing.

OLD SILLTOWN

On the brow of the hill was the home of Andrew Sill, son of Zachariah. It has been described as being two stories high in the front and one story high in the rear, the sides covered with shingles, a commodious home. It is not now standing.

Below the hill was the home of Zachariah. Still farther down the street on a knoll at a bend in the road in 1799 Captain Thomas Sill's home was erected, which is now standing. Across the street from the home of Thomas Sill were the homes of Reuben Tinker, also the Dorr family, ancestors of Edward Dorr Griffin, former president of Williams College, and Mrs. Jaspar Peck, who was Mrs. Phoebe Dorr.

Below Captain Sill's home was that of Captain Joseph Sill, the 4th, who married Miss Elizabeth Lee of Grassy Hill. This house was removed by Mrs. Thomas Sill in her day as being unsightly. However, in the old garden may still be found the old well covered with a stone slab.

There are, at present, two Sill homes left standing in Silltown, all others having disappeared.

The residence of the Sills' farther down the street in Lyme are now owned by other families than those bearing the name Sill.

SILL NEIGHBORS IN SILLTOWN.

History states the neighbors in Silltown in the olden times as being the Dorrs, Wades and Matsons, Edmund Dorr was born in Roxbury, near Boston, in 1692. He was a cloth dresser. He settled in Silltown and established his business on Mill Creek in 1716. He married Miss Mary Griswold of Lyme.

OLD SILLTOWN

The family removed to East Hadam at the time of the Revolutionary War. In 1854 Mrs. George G. Sill, in writing to Mrs. Mary Sill in Silltown, said:

"Opposite your house was the so-called 'My Sarvant Dorr' with his sensible and talented family of children, Edward, who became a minister and settled in Hartford, George, a lawyer and settled in Mantee Parish near Four Mile River, and Matthew, a farmer who lived on the homestead, and his daughter Eve, the mother of Edward Dorr Griffin."

The Wades settled on the same stream and established a millsite farther up the creek.

Nathaniel Matson came from Boston in 1715 and located north of Silltown, dying in 1776, aged 92 years. He was the ancestor of the late Colonel Israel Matson, that greatly esteemed gentleman whose death occurred in 1903. His estate is called "Matson Hill," adjoining Silltown, now the residence of his sister, Mrs. Catherine Ann Matson Terry, and her sons, Charles, Nathaniel and James Luther Terry, M. D., who are known and beloved by the present Old Lyme residents.

A resident in Silltown in the childhood days of the author was Dr. Shubell Bartlett. He came to reside there with his lovely bride, who was Miss Fannie Griswold of Black Hall. She was a delicate blonde with silken curls falling about her face, neck and shoulders, complexion of lily-whiteness, with sparkling hazel eyes. I do not remember having seen her dressed in anything but white. She was my ideal of a beautiful woman. The doctor was a great favorite of my grandfather, and, in fact, with the whole family. He was a frequent visitor at the old colonial home. Dr. Bartlett purchased lands of Captain Thomas Sill (nearly opposite the residence of John

Sill, now belonging to Judge Huntington), and built the home now called "Cricket Lawn." When, in 1849, the gold fever broke out, he went, with others, to the gold fields of California and never returned, having lost his life when crossing "The Isthmus." Professor Charles Bartlett, principal of the Black Hall Preparatory School for young men, is his son.

UPPER MILL.

In Laysville at the outlet of Rogers Lake, near Lyme, north of Silltown, stands a large stone factory, most artistic in appearance, which was owned and operated for many years by Captain Thomas Sill and Deacon Nathaniel Matson in the manufacture of woolen goods. Here were manufactured the Satinet cloth for men's apparel, fine woolen yarns and other

UPPER MILL.

material. Later it was purchased by Mr. Oliver Lay, always called Squire Lay, whose antecedents were the earliest residents of that locality, and after whom the locality was named.

Squire Lay's ancestor, John Lay was one of the first set-

OLD SILLTOWN

tlers in Laysville; tradition states he erected the first house in town on his lands near Duck River. Mr. Daniel Lay, a descendant now living, states that John Lay came from Long Island in 1637. His lands extended from the Connecticut shore on the west to Duck River on the north and to Black Hall River on the east.

DISTINGUISHED DESCENDANTS OF THE SILL FAMILY.

Brigadier General Joshua Woodroe Sill.

Brigadier General Joshua Woodroe Sill, military officer and commander, was born in Chillicothe, Ohio, and graduated

BRIGADIER GENERAL J. W. SILL

in 1854 at the United States Military Academy at West Point with distinguished honors; was professor there until 1857. He was stationed at Ft. Vancouver, Washington Territory, in 1859. He resigned from the army in 1861, re-entering the

OLD SILLTOWN

volunteer service as brigadier general, July 1863. He was killed at the battle of Murfreesboro.

Comte de Paris' History of the Civil War says of him. "Just as Vaughn's troops were beginning to give way, Sill boldly resumed the offensive, chased them at the head of his brigade and drove the enemy back in disorder. But the heroic Sill fell mortally wounded in the battle in the very midst of the enemies' battalions, a victim of his zeal.

Brigadier Gen. Joshua Woodroe Sill was a descendant of Zachariah Sill 1st through Mr. Joseph Sill of Chillicothe, Ohio, of the sixth generation, who graduated from college in 1809 at Montpelier, Vt., studied law with Hon. Cyrus Ware of Montpelier, removed to Philadelphia and was admitted to the bar in 1814. He settled in the practice of his profession at Chillicothe, Ohio; was one of the celebrated lawyers of this, the first capital of Ohio.

His son, Brigadier General Joshua Woodroe Sill, was the idol of the family as well as the community, his name is revered wherever he was known. His body was found after a month of search on the battlefield of Murfreesboro and buried in the beautiful Hills cemetery at Chillicothe, Ohio. Some years ago a man in Texas wrote that he had in his possession General Sill's sword, which he found on the battlefield. He came north with it, presented it to his relatives in Chillicothe, Ohio.

There was a great meeting of war veterans and the Sill Guards, a local company named in his honor; Judge Clifford Douglas, a nephew, received the sword, and presided over the occasion of its presentation. A connection who is not a blood

OLD SILLTOWN

relation in giving this interesting account to the author writes that "the Sill, as well as the Douglas blood, ranks the best in the state and stands for the best in all things."

The daughter of Joseph Sill and sister of Brigadier General Joshua Woodroe Sill was Anna Sill who married when quite young Albert Douglas, whose father, Hon. Richard Douglas, was a noted lawyer of Ohio. Her daughter is Mrs. Stanley Sedgwick of London, England, who is mother of the authoress, Anna Douglas Sedgwick.

The sons of Anna Sill Douglas are the Hon. Albert Douglas, a late member of Congress; Judge Clifford Douglas, who has retired from "The Bench;" Joshua Douglas, living in Buffalo, N. Y., who was named for his uncle.

The only daughter of Anna Sill Douglas was Anna Sill, who still lives unmarried in Princeton, N. J. She is an eminent authority on many subjects. She is in demand by such institutions as the Metropolitan Art Museum of New York, which sends her abroad on missions of investigations of pictures, manuscripts, etc. In her possession is a fine portrait of General Joshua Woodroe Sill, also the general's swords, which are reported to be always hanging crossed above his portrait.

GENERAL MANSFIELD.

General Mansfield, who achieved renown in the Civil War in this country, was a Sill descendant through one Hubbard of Middletown, Conn., who married a Sill. This vigorous old man, at the head of his troops, hastened to reinforce General Hooker at the battle of Antietam, near Durfees Churchyard.

OLD SILLTOWN

ANNA PECK SILL.

A noble representative of the Sill family through Andrew Sill, son of Zachariah Sill, son of Joseph 2nd of Silltown, was Miss Anna Peck Sill. She was born in Burlington, N. Y., August 9, 1816, the youngest of ten children. She inherited

Yours truly,
Anna P Sill

the intellectual and moral qualities of a long line of Puritan ancestry.

In 1849 she operated a school at Rockford, Ill. She set up a standard in the wilderness with a courage that knew no

OLD SILLTOWN

faltering, with a ceaseless vigilance, she patiently, hopefllly, prayerfully wrought out her dream of life. In the year of 1884, after thirty-five years of successful leadership, Miss Sill resigned. She died in her seminary room June 18, 1889. At the alumni reunion Mrs. Matie T. Perry paid her this able tribute:

SILL HALL.

"She was gifted with a wondrous endowment of head and heart and an indomitable will, to carry out her scheme for the betterment of mankind."

Eighth Generation

Henry Sill Hart.

Henry Sill Hart of New York City was a descendant of Captain Joseph Sill through Captain Thos. Sill whose daughter Phoebe, married Mr. C. B. Hart, a prominent citizen of Saybrook, Conn., and descendant of a family of that town. Henry Sill Hart died in February, 1903, aged 78 years. The Brooklyn Eagle states of him: "He was especially endeared to his friends for his sterling qualities." He was born in East Hadam, Conn. His early childhood was passed in Lyme. He removed to Utica and was in the employ of his uncle, Mr. A. L. Welles in the retail dry goods business. He removed to New York City and became well-known there in dry goods circles as a resident buyer for western jobbing houses. He continued in this business for the remainder of his life. He was always actively interested in the general development of every enterprise which tended to promote the general interests of New York City as a dry goods market. He was a member and director of the Brooklyn Club and also a member of the Union League, Marine and Field Club of Brooklyn and a member of the Merchants Club of Manhattan, also a member of the New England Society. All of these organizations contained devoted friends of many years' standing and his death was recognized to be a severe loss to acquaintances, friends, relatives and the community at large. Mr. Hart had always been a good friend to Mrs. Mary Sill who, for so many years,

HENRY SILL HART.

lived alone in the Thomas Sill homestead in Silltown. To her he always gladly extended sympathy and assistance and upon her death he became owner of the property.

OLD SILLTOWN

THOMAS HALE SILL.

Thomas Hale Sill of Erie, Pennsylvania, a descendant of the line of Richard Sill, the 1st, of Saybrook, Conn., was attorney general of the United States in 1819.

Rev. Frederick Shrader Sill of Cohoes, N. Y., born New York City, 1848. Graduate of Stephen's College, 1869 and

REVEREND FREDERICK SHRADER SILL.

General Theological Seminary, 1872. Deacon, 30th June, 1872. Priest, 21st September, 1873. Registrar of Diocese of Albany. Archdeacon of Albany. Rector of St. John's Church, Cohoes, N. Y. Married, February 6th., 1879, to Mary Power.

OLD SILLTOWN

He is a descendant of Thomas Sill of Middletown, Conn., and of Joseph Sill the 1st. He is a gifted minister of the Episcopal Church. He has three sons; his namesake, Frederick DeVeter, is a civil engineer employed in the construction of the Panama Canal, and has been thus engaged for three years (1910).

THOMAS HENRY SILL.

Thomas Henry Sill of New York, died April 6th, 1909. Established a mission in a neglected region of the city near 39th street, and after many years of good service, he had the satisfaction of seeing a church erected in that neighborhood which was completed shortly before his death. He was vicar in charge for forty-four years. At the time of his death he was the oldest clergyman of any sort in office. He was a descendant of Thomas Sill of Connecticut. His eldest son, Henry A. Sill, graduated from Columbia College, New York, in 1888, studied at Oxford, England, and at the University of Halle from 1893 to 1900, and took his P. H. D. there under Professor Meyer. He has been a professor in the History Department at Cornell University for several years. Another son of Thomas Sill of New York was Reverend Frederick H. Sill, best known as Father Sill, who was also a graduate of Columbia College, New York, in 1895. He was ordained to the ministry as Deacon in 1898 and as Priest in 1899. He has been a member for many years of the order of the Holy Cross in the Episcopal Church. He started a school for boys at Kent, Conn., in 1906, of which he is head master.

OLD SILLTOWN

Another son of Thomas Sill is James B. Sill, also a graduate of Columbia College in 1892. Became Deacon in the Episcopal Church in 1897 and Priest in 1898 in the diocese of New York. Was connected with the Church of the Redeemer for several years, afterwards a missionary in the diocese of Albany, New York.

EDWARD ROWLAND SILL.

Edward Rowland Sill, a descendant of Elisha Sill of Windsor, Conn., a gifted writer of both poetry and prose and whose death was greatly mourned. It is said of him: "Edward Rowland Sill stood very high in breadth of thought and falicity of expression; he, in his writings, pours forth lavishly the treasures of heart and head."

EDWARD EVERETT SILL.

Edward Everett Sill, formerly of New Haven, now of New York, an active member of "Order of the Founders and Patriots" of Hartford, whose eulogy on the Reverend Stephen Johnson, delivered some time ago at one of the anniversaries of this society in Hartford, gave due credit to that fine old patriot. We quote it:

"History says there were many genuine patriots in the early days of the colonies. Among them was the Reverend Stephen Johnson of Lyme, Conn. He took up the side of liberty about ten years before the Revolutionary War broke out, at the time of the infamous Stamp Act. He wrote essays for the Connecticut Gazette, published in New London, and sent them secretly to the printer. Three or four of them were published and the eyes of the people began to open, and when war did come, Mr. Johnson had the satisfaction of seeing patriotic and faithful men engaged in the service of the colonies, and went himself as chaplain when Boston was the seat of war."

ELISHA MATHER SILL.

Elisha Mather Sill, M. D., of New York City, is a descendant of Captain Joseph Sill through Joseph Sill the 2nd, through Dr. Elisha Sill who settled in Goshen, Conn. Elisha Mather Sill is prominent in medical circles and a member of many medical societies.

HERBERT RALPH SILL.

Herbert Ralph Sill, son of Charles Henry Sill (descendant of Thomas Sill of Middletown, Conn., son of Joseph Sill the 2nd of Lyme), resides at Bayonne, N. Y., is interested in a Spanish firm and has large interests in Brazil and South America.

HOWARD SILL.

Howard Sill of Baltimore, Md., is a descendant of Captain Joseph Sill in the following order:
Howard Mather Sill, son of
Judge William Nicol Sill, son of
Major Richard Sill, son of
Lieut. John Sill, son of
Joseph Sill, son of
Captain Joseph Sill

Mr. Howard Sill has collected much data concerning the family.

OLD SILLTOWN

MAJOR GENERAL ALFRED ELLIOT BATES, U. S. A.

Major General Alfred Elliot Bates, U. S. A., a distinguished descendant of Captain Joseph Sill, 1st, was Major General Alfred Elliot Bates, U. S. A. His line of descent comes through Joseph 2nd, who removed to North Lyme. Jabez, the fourth son of Joseph 2nd, married Elizabeth Noyes, daughter of Rev. Moses of Lyme, the first pastor of the First Church of Christ. Their daughter, Mary Sill, married James Gould of North Lyme and their daughter, Sarah, married Phineas P. Bates, whose son, Alfred Gould Bates, married Betsy Ann Elliot. Major General Bates was their son.

He was born in 1840 and was graduated from West Point in 1865. In 1869 he married Caroline McCorkle. After serving in the west, where he distinguished himself as an Indian fighter, he was appointed as instructor at West Point, but took the field again in 1874 and was in the Big Horn expedition. In command of a troop of cavalry, with two hundred Shoshone Indians, he defeated the Arapahoes at Snake Mountain. In 1875 he went on the staff as Paymaster General U. S. A. In 1898 he was appointed military attache at the Court of St. James. He was retired January 22, 1904, as Major General U. S. A., a rank conferred upon him by Secretary Elihu Root, in recognition of his long and unusually meritorious service to his department.

In May, 1906, he was sent to San Francisco to look after the accounting of the Red Cross and Government funds contributed for the relief of earthquake sufferers.

He is survived by Mrs. Bates to whom I am indebted for the accompanying portrait of the general taken in London.

OLD SILLTOWN

His two daughters, Mrs. F. R. Swift and Mrs. M. D. McKee of 162 East Seventy-fourth street and two sisters, Mrs.

MAJOR GENERAL ALFRED ELLIOTT BATES, U. S. A.

Wellington and Mrs. William Laurence of 969 Fifth avenue, New York City, have kindly furnished the writer with this record of the general's eventful life.

MAJOR GENERAL JAMES FRANKLIN WADE, U. S. A.

Another illustrious descendant, now living, is Major General James Franklin Wade, U. S. A.

His line of descent was as follows—as taken from the Register of Members and Ancestors for 1901 of the Society of Colonial Wars in the State of Minnesota:

Captain Joseph Sill 1639-1696 married
Sarah (Clark) Marvin, their son
Joseph Sill 1687 married
Phoebe Lord 1686, their daughter
Sarah Sill 1728-1814 married
Nehimiah Hubbard 1721-1814, their son
Colonel Nehimiah Hubbard 1753-1834 married
Cornelia Willis 1754-1781, their daughter
Sarah Hubbard 1780-1862 married
Depire Roseneraus, their daughter
Caroline M. Roseneraus 1805-1889 married
Benjamin Franklin Wade 1800-1878 and
Major General James Franklin Wade, U. S. A., is their son.

He served in the Civil War, the Cuban War, and the Philippine War. He was a graduate of West Point and his service covers the period from 1861 to 1907, over forty-six years.

James Franklin Wade, Major General, U. S. A., son of Benjamin T. Wade, senator from Ohio, was born in Jefferson, Ohio, April 14, 1843. When eighteen years of age he was appointed First Lieutenant of the 6th U. S. Cavalry from

Very truly yours

OLD SILLTOWN

Ohio in 1861, Lieutenant Colonel U. S. Cavalary, May 1, 1864, Brigadier General 1864, entered the regular United States Army 1866 as Major 9th Cavalry, Lieutenant Colonel 1897, Brigadier General 1897, Major General 1898, Major General U. S. A., 1903, and was commander of Atlantic Division in 1904.

He rendered gallant and meritorious service at the battle of Beverly Ford, Va.; at Marion, East Tennessee in the campaign in southwestern Virginia in the Civil War in 1865.

He was head of the Cuban Evacuation Committee in 1898, served in the Philippines in 1901, commanded a division in the Philippines in 1903-4.

Major General Wade resides in Jefferson, Ashtabula County, Ohio. His photograph, kindly donated to the author by the general himself, presents his fine presence and apparent health, prosperity and happiness.

OLD SILLTOWN

FINAL.

This volume contains a record of events obtained from a great variety of sources as mentioned in the preface. Various items have been supplied from time to time by connections, descendants and friends of the family, a few of whom are now living and some of whom are now dead. The nature of the text of this volume implies absolute certainty of statement where dates and events are positively matters of record and are therefore authentic or when the events recorded are matters of tradition or observation by the writer or by those whom the writer has known in their lifetime, the text again so implies. The records and histories of the progenitors of the family testify to their sterling worth of character, also their refinement and their religious zeal. They were men of position, of learning and of means. They were devoted to the church of which they were members and interested in establishing a government and schools, of protecting their institutions of liberty and in giving of their means to the interests of their town or community. They leave us a priceless heritage of uprightness and honor. It remains for us, their descendants, to maintain this high standard and ever to bear in mind the example thus set before us. We would not claim for them perfection or infallibility, but it was their general desire to live godly, brave and virtuous lives and to establish government of civil and religious liberty in their native land in which their early ancestor had established the family.

The Sill enclosure in Duck River Cemetery in Lyme conserves the bodies of over thirty of these ancestors, those descending through the oldest son, Joseph the 1st, representing eight generations.

OLD SILLTOWN

At the solicitation of Sarah Welles Burt their resting place has been suitably enclosed, many headstones have been reset, names which were about to be obliterated by time, have been re-cut and a marble slab has been placed over the tomb of Captain Joseph Sill, which gives an indication of his record of services. In doing this the ancient headstones have not been disturbed but have been preserved for posterity. On a cornerstone of the enclosure is inscribed "Erected by the Sill Family."

As attesting to the general interest of the present living generations of descendants in the restoration and preservation of the old Sill family lot, we here record as completely as possible, the names of those who contributed:

Richard Townsend Peckham
John S. Peckham
William Peckham
Mrs. Maria Martin
Louisa Peckham
Josephine Welles Richardson
Mr. Henry Hart
Frank Sill Rogers, Albany, N. Y.
Mr. Richard Hart
Mr. William Sill
Mr. William Welles
Mr. Samuel Welles
Miss Nettie Sill
Mrs. Mary Hart-Pixley
Mr. George Sill Welles
Mrs. George Sill Welles
Miss Mary Pixley

Mr. George Sill
Mrs. Mary Sill
Rev. Frederick Sill
Mrs. Amelia Huntington Sill
Miss Leonora Sill
Mrs. Sarah Louisa Newton Hickox
Mr. Edward Everett Sill
Mrs. S. M. Sill Burt, Hartford, Conn.
Mrs. Harriet Baldwin Davidson, Jamaica, L. I.
Miss Caroline Baldwin, Middletown, Conn.
Mr. Henry Sill Baldwin, Middletown, Conn.
Miss Carrie Eyke Sill, Hartford, Conn.
Dr. John Sill, Argyle, N. Y.
Mary Sill Snow, Old Saybrook
Fanny M. Sill
Jennie A. Sill
Sarah E. Sill
Charles A. Sill
Mrs. Jennie M. Peck
Mrs. A. P. Simpson
Mr. John Sill, Ashtabula, Ohio
Mrs. Sarah Hart Bradley
Mr. Clinton Bradley
Mr. Harry Bradley
Mrs. Sarah H. Taylor
Miss Selden, Erie, Penn.
Major General James F. Wade, U. S. A.
Lieut. John P. Wade, U. S. A.
Mrs. S. Laurence
Dr. John C. Sill

OLD SILLTOWN

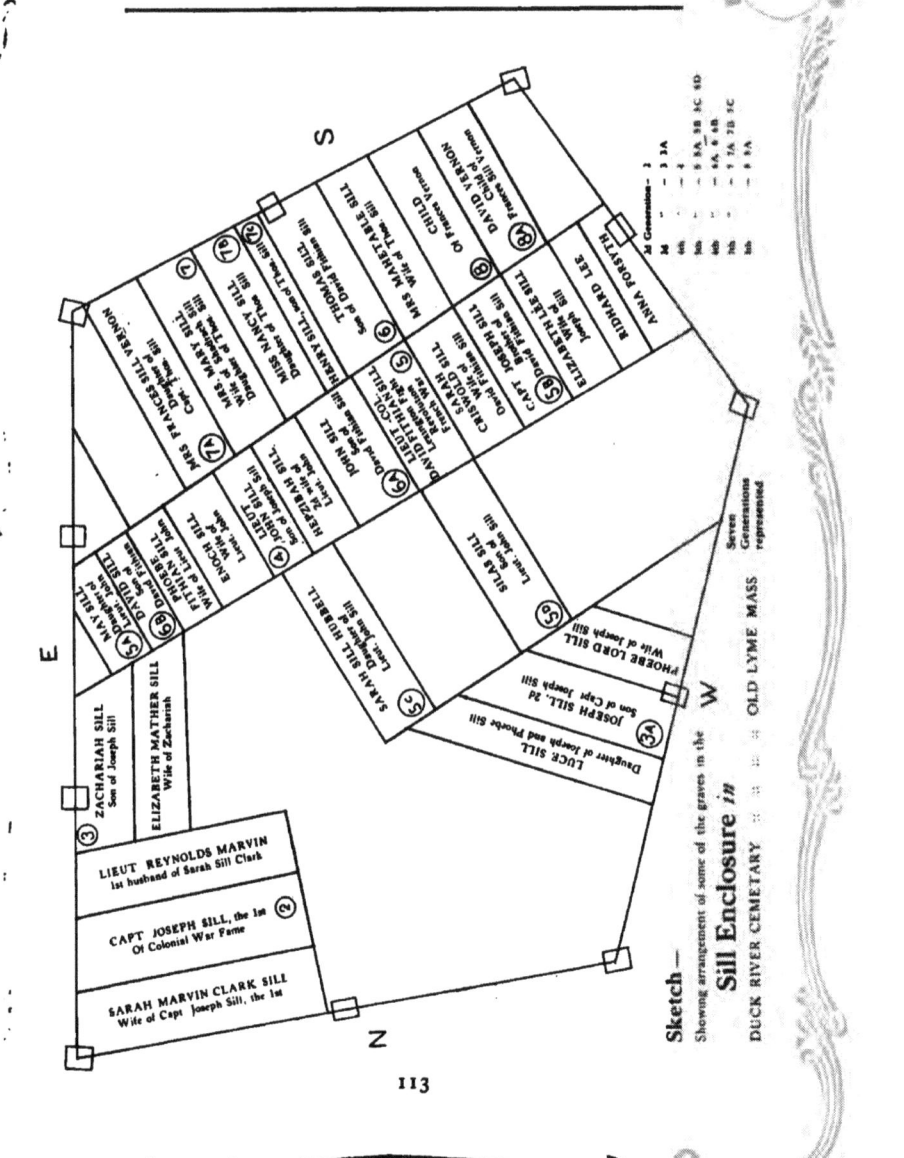

Sketch—
Showing arrangement of some of the graves in the
Sill Enclosure *in*
DUCK RIVER CEMETARY :: :: :: OLD LYME MASS

Seven Generations represented

1st Generation — 2
2d — 3, 3A
3d — 5, 5A, 5B, 5C, 5D
4th — 4A, 6, 6B
5th — 7, 7A, 7B, 9C
6th — 8
8 — 9A

(2) CAPT JOSEPH SILL, the 1st
Of Colonial War Fame

SARAH MARVIN CLARK SILL
Wife of Capt Joseph Sill, the 1st

LIEUT REYNOLDS MARVIN
1st husband of Sarah Sill Clark

(3) ZACHARIAH SILL
Son of Joseph Sill

ELIZABETH MATHER SILL
Wife of Zachariah

(3A) JOSEPH SILL, 2d
Son of Capt Joseph Sill

LUCE SILL
Daughter of Joseph and Phoebe Sill

PHOEBE LORD SILL
Wife of Joseph Sill

(5C) David ... Sill
Lieut John Sill

SARAH SILL HUBBELL
Lieut ... Sill

SILAS SILL
Lieut John Sill

(5) MARETABLE SILL
Wife of Thos. Sill

THOMAS SILL
Son of David Fisher

MRS NANCY SILL
Daughter of Thos ...

HENRY SILL
...

(4) LIEUT JOHN SILL
Son of Joseph Sill

HEZIBIAH SILL
2d Wife of John
Lieut of John

DAVID COMST...
...

CHRISTOPHER SILL
...

SARAH HOAD SILL
Wife of ...

Capt JOSEPH SILL
...

ELIZABETH SILL
...

RICHARD LEE
ANNA GOODALE

DAVID VERNON
Frances Sill Vernon

Child of Frances P Sill

MRS MARY SILL
Wife of Shadrach Sill

MRS FRANCES SILL VERNON
Daughter of Capt ...

DAVID ...
son of ...

PHOEBE SILL
Wife of John
1st Lieut John Sill

ENOCH SILL
Son of John
Lieut John ...

MARVIN SILL
David ...

113

OLD SILLTOWN

Helen Sill, Argyle, N. Y.
Sarah Seldon, descendant of Anna Sill
Florence Virginia Sill
William Griswold Burt
Mrs. Sarah Sill Welles Burt

On Memorial Day the flag of our country is placed to wave over the graves of Captain Joseph Sill and Colonel David Fithian Sill; thus, though years have passed, the Colonial and Revolutionary soldiers are not forgotten. May their memory be ever kept fresh by descendants of present and future generations. We here take the liberty of quoting from "The Hidden Village" by Hamilton Mabee, in 1908, which appropriately may preceed the final illustration in this volume:

> "The ancient churchyard lies in the very lap of nature and has been cherished into a touching and tender loveliness of ripe age. The paths between the graves are sweet with memorial turf so that the living are as quiet as the dead in this sacred place. The stones are gray with age and time has erased the names of those that sleep below; in a general beneficence that enfolds the place there is no need of individual remembrance. They that sleep are

OLD SILLTOWN

enfolded by a great blessedness of peace. Centuries ago they went out of the tumult and the storm and are now at rest in this sweet haven!"

SILL ENCLOSURE, IN DUCK RIVER CEMETERY, OLD LYME, CONN.

OLD SILLTOWN

INTERESTING REMINISCENCES OF OLD LYME AND INDIVIDUALS AND EVENTS CONNECTED WITH OLD LYME.

OLD LYME STORE USED FOR STORING AMMUNITION AFTER THE WAR OF 1812.

An interesting instant in connection with Lyme and its history about the year 1812 was related to the writer by Mr. Chas. Harvey of Marquette, Mich. Mr. Harvey was a man of world-wide reputation and public benefactor for he invented and constructed the first elevated railroad in New York City, and his wife was the first lady who rode on it. In northern Michigan he engineered and constructed the canal and locks, at Sault Ste. Marie the semi-centennial celebration of which occurred in 1905 in which the then Vice-President Fairbanks and prominent Canadian officials took part. Mr. Harvey was born in the town of Colchester, parish of North Chester, and was a native of Connecticut. He was the son of a Congregational minister who afterwards became a Presbyterian and established the First Presbyterian Church in Connecticut, which is now the large Theological Seminary in Hartford. His son Charles, as a youth in 1840 was offered a position (which he accepted) with John Hart's store in Lyme, Conn., which was situated at the lower end of the main street of Lyme on the green, opposite Squire McCurdy's home. This store was about 200 feet to the right of being directly in front of where Dr. Griffin's house stands. Mr. Harvey was an own cousin of the late Chief Justice Waite of the Supreme Court of the United States, their mothers being sisters, the Misses Selden of Hadlyme. While in John Hart's employ, Charles

OLD SILLTOWN

Harvey undertook the renovation of the cellar of the store and there, deeply buried in an accumulation of debris, he found a quantity of cannon balls, the story of them being as follows:

"During the war of 1812 a fleet of British vessels came up the Sound and anchored off the mouth of the Connecticut River. At that time both the towns of Essex and Lyme (especially Essex) were noted for being the centers of shipping industries and it was the purpose of the British to destroy the shipyards in these places. They accordingly equipped an expedition for this purpose. They embarked from their men-of-war and rowed up the river to Essex where they burned part of the town and all of the shipping. (At the present time the remains of an old hulk which was burned to the water's edge and sunk may be seen at Essex and visitors can be shown the old fire place in an old colonial house near the river, from which live coals were taken to start the conflagration in the shipyards.)

"In the meantime the citizens of Lyme had made preparation for defense. They called their men together and placed a field gun with ammunition on the top of Hoyes Hill overlooking the river. They discerned, however, that the British forces were much stronger than their own and concluded that to begin action would surely draw upon Lyme an attack by the British and, therefore, concluded they would begin action only after being attacked. Accordingly the British boats passed quietly down the river without so much as a gun having been fired by the Lyme men."

Thus, the cannon balls which had been provided come to be stored in the basement of John Hart's store, and there remained until Mr. Harvey found them, as stated above.

OLD SILLTOWN

CONCERNING MRS. MATTHEW GRISWOLD.

The following is a copy of a clipping taken from the Deep River New Era:

A CENTENNIAL ANNIVERSARY.

Mrs. Matthew Griswold Passes the Century Mark.

An event of unusual interest to all in our community, and indeed to many not citizens of our town, took place on Sunday, July 17th, 1904. An esteemed resident of Old Lyme, Mrs. Matthew Griswold, of Black Hall, reached the good round age of 100 years. Probably never in the history of Old Lyme, nor in the history of the several municipalities which are its neighbors, and which were once comprehended as the town of Lyme, has a citizen reached so ripe an age.

Mrs. Griswold was born in Lyme in the township north of the present town of Old Lyme, July 17th, 1804. It may, therefore, be said that during her whole life she has been a resident of the same town. Mrs. Griswold was the daughter of Col. Seth Ely. Her birthplace has always been known as Mount Archer.

On July 5th, 1827, she was married to Mr. Matthew Griswold, and the Griswold homestead at Black Hall (which has for more than two centuries been the birthplace of men eminent in affairs of town and state), has ever since been her home.

To Mr. and Mrs. Griswold eight children were born, all of whom were daughters except one. Seven children are now living. One daughter died some years ago. The son, Mr. Matthew Griswold, lives at Erie, Pa., and conducts a very successful manufacturing business in that city. For several terms he was a member of Congress from Pennsylvania.

Mrs. Griswold united with the Old Lyme Congregational Church in April, 1828. It is doubtful if in any church in our state or even in our country is to be found a living member whose membership antedates hers.

To the busy bustling outside world, it might appear that Mrs. Griswold's life has been uneventful. She has been wont in her modest way to speak of it in such terms herself. But it has been a life strong, dignified, gentle and influential for the things true, venerable, just, pure, lovely and of good report, and no one who has come in contact with it but has gone out into the world a better man or a better woman for its fellowship. The whole community gladly honors this noble woman of Christian character and experience and wishes for her remaining days on earth freedom from bodily pain and the peace that cometh from Him whom she has loved and served for so many years.

What a history hers has been. She has lived through a century, than which the world has not seen one more wonderful, a century which has been nothing short of miraculous in the several realms in which man lives and moves and has his being.

Until within a few months, Mrs. Griswold has enjoyed excellent health. Though now somewhat weak bodily, she is full as well as could be expected and quietly awaits in the midst of her loving family the homeward call.

About four months later to be followed by:

"Mrs. Matthew Griswold died at her home in Black Hall on Saturday, November 26th, at the unusual age of 100 years

OLD SILLTOWN

and four months. Mrs. Griswold was born at Mt. Archer, North Lyme, in 1804 and in 1827 was married to Matthew Griswold, son of Gov. Roger Griswold. Her maiden name was Ely. Mrs. Griswold had never known illness during her whole long life and retained her faculties almost to the end. Her death came from advanced age. Mrs. Griswold was the mother of eight children, four of whom lived with her at the old family place. Her oldest daughter died some years ago. She leaves to mourn her death six daughters, one of whom is Mrs. J. C. Selden of Erie, Pa., and Mrs. H. S. Ely of New York City, and one son, Matthew Griswold of Erie, Pa., a prominent business man and founder of the Griswold Manufacturing Company of that place. Her funeral was attended by many friends on Tuesday afternoon from her residence in Black Hall.

The funeral of Phoebe H. Ely Griswold, widow of Matthew Griswold, took place at her late home at Black Hall on Tuesday afternoon. The deceased was in her one hundred and

GRISWOLD BURYING GROUND, BLACK HALL, CONN.

first year and many persons gathered to pay their last respects. Numerous handsome floral pieces attested the sorrowful remembrance of her friends. Rev. Chas. Villiers was the officiating clergyman. Interment was in the Griswold burying ground at Black Hall. The bearers were five grandsons and a grand nephew of the deceased woman. They were Wm. Griswold, Roger Wolcott Griswold, Dwight Griswold, Horace Griswold Ely, Matthew Griswold Ely and Chas. Griswold Bartlett.

CONCERNING MRS. GERTRUDE McCURDY GRIFFIN.

FROM THE DEEP RIVER NEW ERA.

In our last issue we announced the death of Mrs. G. McCurdy Griffin at her home in Old Lyme on Wednesday, September 14th, 1904. The news of her death which came with great surprise to all who heard of it, brought sadness to many hearts in the community and far beyond it. Though perhaps not quite in her usual health, she was, on the morning of her decease, well and cheerful, and in conversation with members of her family within a few moments of her departure from the home which had been hers from birth to the land which has no shadows. Gertrude McCurdy Lord, daughter of Stephen J. Lord, and Sarah Ann McCurdy was born at Old Lyme, March 5th, 1840. Her education begun at Mrs. Phoebe Griffin Noyes' School, Old Lyme, was continued at Miss Drapers' School in Hartford, and at Miss Haines' School at New York City. At all these institutions she ranked high in general scholarship, and especially so in higher mathematics. In September, 1856, she became a member of the Congregational Church, the church of many of her ancestors, and with which from childhood, she had been associated. She was married on June 11th, 1862, to Dr. Edward Dorr Griffin, son of George Griffin and Ann Augusta Neilson of Catskill, N. Y. Dr. Griffin, a product of the College of Physicians and Surgeons in New York, practiced medicine in Old Lyme until his death, some twenty-two years later. Mrs. Griffin loved her church dearly, and always gave of her means, her time and her thought, of herself, to promote in every way its interests. She took a deep and vital interest in missions, at home and abroad. Of quiet nature, a devoted love of her home and family, she nevertheless as a Christian woman did her part in whatever ways she could, for the material, mental and moral welfare of the community. Of superior intelligence, her reading was both wide and varied, but the book she loved and studied above all others, was the Bible. In it she found, while reading it for devotional ends, true nourishment for mind and spirit. To those who knew Mrs. Griffin best—knew her as one friend knows another—the impression made upon their minds, through their acquaintance with her, was that she was a woman of great sincerity, of deep sympathy and of remarkable serenity. Truly, her fellowship was with God, and the result was a life and character quiet, gentle and gracious.

MRS. CATHARINE MATSON TERRY.
ARTICLE FROM THE DEEP RIVER NEW ERA, NOVEMBER 1ST, 1912.

Mrs. Catharine Matson Terry, widow of Rev. James Pease Terry, died at her home, Matson Hill, Lyme, on Tuesday afternoon, October 29, in the 90th year of her age. She was the only daughter of Israel Matson and Phoebe Ely Matson.

She was born at Lyme January 28th, 1823. At an early age she attended school at New London and later at Mrs. Apthorp's school for girls on Hillhouse avenue, New Haven. She married Rev. James P. Terry, who was pastor of the Congregational church at Somers, Conn. Later they moved to South Weymouth, Mass., where Mr. Terry was pastor of the Second Congregational church for over thirty years.

After Mr. Terry's death in 1873 Mrs. Terry lived at her old home in Lyme. She then moved to Philadelphia and made her home there with two of her sons, Dr. J. L. Terry and Frank A. Terry, until about two years ago when she and her son, Dr. Terry, returned to Lyme.

She was a woman of exceptional mental attainments and beautiful Christian character. She was beloved by all who knew her and her long life was filled with unselfish devotion to others.

Her brother, Nathaniel Matson, was graduated at Yale college in the class of 1847. He died at Hartford in 1851. Her youngest brother, Col. Israel Matson, with whom she lived at Lyme after her husband's death, was on the staff of his cousin, Governor Buckingham, during the Civil War.

Her children now living are Prof. N. M. Terry of the naval academy at Annapolis, Dr. J. L. Terry of Lyme, Frank A. Terry of Philadelphia, Pa., and Charles A. Terry of New York. Her son, Rev. I. N. Terry, D. D., died in 1908 at Utica, N. Y., where he was for several years pastor of the Westminster Presbyterian church.

Mrs. Terry's memory will be cherished by all of her many

friends because of her cheerful disposition, her self-sacrificing devotion to her family and her townspeople, and her noble character.

Mrs. Terry united with the First Congregational church of Old Lyme in September, 1838, and although her membership was afterward removed to other churches of which her husband was pastor, she retained a warm interest in the church of her youth, and was able to attend its services within a few weeks of her death. She entered the church under the ministry of the Rev. Chester Colton and was probably the only survivor of those who united with this church prior to the pastorate of the Rev. D. S. Brainerd. A woman of high faith and genuine piety, her presence was an inspiration to her fellow Christians to the end.

Funeral services were conducted by the Rev. E. M. Chapman at her home on October 31st. Interment was in the family burial plot in Old Lyme cemetery. The pallbearers were Thomas B. Farwell, George Griswold, Waldo Banning and John E. Noyes.

Memorial Discourse

of the

First Congregational Church
1693-1876

of

Old Lyme, Connecticut

July 19th, 1876

By
WM. B. CARY

Discourse

In the wonderful disposition of Providence, it has fallen to me—a stranger to Lyme six months ago, yet, by descent, a rightful participant in all that pertains to her history—it has fallen to me to prepare and deliver a memorial discourse from this time-hallowed pulpit.

What a stranger-hand might but mechanically touch in tracing the history of this church, thrills me with concern and delight as from the yellow, time-worn record page the events of the past have been discovered to me, for in this place my maternal ancestors had their birth, and from here went forth to fight in the War of Independence.

If, in the pleasure of Almighty God, your late pastor had been spared to this Centennial year, this church would have had a historical discourse rich in reminiscence and full in detail. Wanting his varied learning and wide experience, and depending upon the meagre notices preserved in town, society, and church records, and some well-preserved traditions, I still find a wealth of history that with pride may be cherished by this church to the last generations.

ORGANIZATION OF THE CHURCH.

An old record reads thus: "Lyme, Mch. the 27th, 1693, at a town meeting it was desired and agreed upon with the inhabitants of this town, as agreed by a unanimous vote, that there may be a church gathered in this town, and Mr. Noyes called to office, if it may be obtained according to the rules of Christ."

OLD SILLTOWN

"Ye prime Society of Lyme" was thus organized, and the Rev. Moses Noyes was installed its pastor. He had, however, been preaching to the people of Lyme for twenty-seven years prior to this, or from the year 1666, nor does it appear why a church was not earlier organized. The unsettled state of society at that time, when the fathers were attempting a settlement among wild and jealous tribes of Indians, may account for it. Preaching, however, was sustained by the people of the new settlement which took the name of Lyme.

MEETING-HOUSES BUILT.

A meeting-house was built shortly after Mr. Noyes began to preach, probably, before 1668. Tradition describes it as a small log-house erected by the settlers on the brow of meeting-house hill, overlooking the Sound and the surrounding country.

The old Indian trail crossed the hill at this place, and it was by this worn pathway that the men on horseback with the women on pillions behind them, came to meeting.

How the aged eyes of the grandfathers lighted up with excitement, and the hot blood of youth came again to the sunken cheeks as they described the scenes of those days! The men came with their loaded muskets in their hands, and regularly detailed some of their number to stand guard during the services that they might not be surprised by the Indians.

The women, by their courageous devotion in sharing privation and braving peril, sustained their husbands and sons in the laudable design of planting a settlement and a church here.

OLD SILLTOWN

In this primitive house the early settlers held their meetings for about twenty-one years, or until 1689, when the second meeting-house was built. This date appears to be well authenticated from the following minute of the appointment by the general court, of a committee to locate the house, and their report there upon.

This committee visited Lyme and heard the "several allegations and reasons" of the people, and "saw reason to pitch upon two places where to set the meeting-house, and with the consent of the greatest part of the people of Lyme, we, after calling upon the Lord, commended the decision of the case to a lot, which lot fell upon the southernmost we had appointed, which is upon the hill where the now meeting-house stands, more northerly, in the very place where we shall stake it out." The report is signed by Jno. Talcott, Jno. Allin.

"This day in Lyme, June 4th, 1686."

Also the following minute on the records of the town.

"September the 26th, 1695, at the same meeting, Joseph Peck demanded of the town £2, 19s. 06d., due to him when the new meeting-house was built in the year 1689." Which records establish the fact that there was a meeting-house standing before this one was built, and that this one was built in the year 1689.

It was a commodious and substantial building capable of accommodating all the inhabitants of the town.

Its location was on the brow of the hill, somewhat to the north and west of the first one, and on the other side of the Indian trail, which had by this time developed into a well-worn track for horses.

OLD SILLTOWN

The brow of the hill was chosen as a site for the second house for the same reason probably, as before, viz.: On account of its security from surprise by the Indians; also, because it was midway between the settlements at Blackhall and the region now called Whippoorwill, and the town of Saybrook, opposite to which, on the banks of the Great River, was another growing settlement that demanded church accommodations.

After thirty-eight years of service it seems this house needed some repairs. On the Society records of January 4th, 1727, there is this minute in the quaint old language of the times, "It was voted yt they will repair ye meeting-house in manner and form as follows: First, to clabord ye fore side of said hows, and part of ye east end, and rectifie ye windows and glass, and what els ye cometee for yt affair think fit, not exceeding forty pounds."

In the year 1734, the second house was found to be too small to accommodate the increasing population, consequently, we find a record to this effect, "Voted, that this Society think it highly necessary, and convenient to erect or build a new meeting-house in this Society." And the next year the Society voted to build a house "60ft. long by 40ft. wide, and 24ft. between the sill and the plate," and a committee was appointed to go to the General Court and ask the appointment of a committee by that body to locate the site for it, inasmuch as the Society could not agree upon any among themselves, and as the former committee had acted so judiciously and well.

The site selected was still the brow of the hill, a little to the north and west of the old house.

OLD SILLTOWN

After the second meeting-house had stood forty-nine years, we find by the Society records in 1738, the third meeting-house was inclosed, and a committee was appointed to finish it. There is also the following minute: "Sept. the 19th, 1738. Voted, that this Society will pull down the old meeting-house, and improve what timber and boards that will be proper towards finishing the new meeting-house in this Society."

It was not burned down as some tradition has it, nor worn out, but was inadequate to the wants of the increasing population.

The third house was located on the same hill as the second, and a short distance from it. And from the fact that this same site was chosen, it is apparent that the interests of the people, settled on the bottom lands between meeting-house hills and the Connecticut river were so important as to demand consideration, as, otherwise, the meeting-house would have been located nearer to Blackhall.

In 1754, one Barnabas Tuthill offered to give a bell to the Society if the people would build a steeple for it to hang in. A steeple was accordingly built, and the first bell began to summon the people to meeting, in lieu of the horn or trumpet, which, tradition says, they had been accustomed to hear.

This bell rang in the Independence of the Colonies in Lyme, and in default of any record as to its final disposition, I suggest the probability that it was given, with others throughout the Colonies, to make cannon for the Revolution; for in the year 1780, the Society voted "to procure a bell for the steeple," thus signifying that the old one had been disposed of in some way. I do not offer it as a historical fact, but make the suggestion that the bell was melted up for war purposes.

This same year, 1780, the third meeting-house caught fire in the roof from the tow wad of the old-fashioned flint-lock musket which one of the guardians of the house used to shoot some woodpeckers that were boring holes in it. The fire was extinguished by the light horsemen stationed in the town—or, as tradition says, by the Hessians, who clambered on the roof like squirrels. The Society voted $100 on this occasion, "to such persons as dangerously exerted themselves to extinguish the late fire."

In the year 1815, after standing 76 years, this house was struck by lightning and burned to the ground, very little of the material being saved.

The present meeting-house, the fourth built by this Society, was erected in 1817, near the south end of the main street. A model of architectural beauty in those days, a beautiful and graceful building for any age.

The corner-stone was laid in 1816, with imposing ceremonies, a copper plate being deposited in it, inscribed as follows:

> "Old meeting-house burnt by
> lightning, July 3, A. D. 1815.
> This corner-stone laid with
> religious ceremonies by the
> Rev. Lathrop Rockwell, Pastor,
> June 10th, A. D. 1816.
> Sam. Belcher, Architect.
> Eben Smith, Master mason."

THE OLD CHURCH AT LYME, PAINTING BY CHILDE HASSAM.

OLD SILLTOWN

The names of the building committee were inscribed on the other side of the plate. The house was seated at first with the old-fashioned square pews at the sides, and "slips" in the center.

The first pulpit was a high, circular one, reached by a flight of steps from either side. Those who remember it describe it as a beautiful and costly mahogany pulpit, and lament its destruction. In 1836 it was first lowered. In 1850 it was removed altogether, and a high platform was built, and the present pulpit set upon it. At the same time, the square pews were removed, and the modern ones substituted in their stead.

The church was at first surrounded by a picket fence, which was repaired from time to time, but was finally removed.

In one corner of the church yard stood that old relic of primitive times, the whipping-post; the indispensable ornament of every New England village. But all traces of it have long since vanished, and the present generation has fortunately only the memory of it, not the fact.

The stocks were erected on the opposite side of the main street, but the memory of the oldest inhabitant serves only to recall their use as a plaything for the boys.

The present church has stood sixty-one years, and is now in an excellent state of preservation.

These grand old elms that so beautify and adorn the church yard, were planted in the year 1828, when the Society appointed a committee "to procure ornamental trees to set about the meeting-house."

OLD SILLTOWN

If we have to thank the fathers for anything, we surely have to for this beneficent act. He who plants a tree scarcely realizes the bounty of his deed; future generations will rise up and call him blessed.

The aggregate number of years that this town has had a meeting-house for the worship of God, is 208, although the society is but 183 years old.

THE PASTORS.

In its 183 years of life, the Society has had eight pastors. And in reviewing the record, the observer is struck by the conviction that it has been wonderfully blessed in the selection.

First is the veteran founder of the Society, Moses Noyes, a faithful minister to Lyme for twenty-seven years of the infant life of the settlement, and afterwards, pastor of the church for twenty-eight years.

The best blood of England was the best blood of America; well illustrated in the case of Moses Noyes, who was the son of James Noyes of Wiltshire, who was the son of William Noyes of Salisbury, who was Attorney General of England from about 1608 till after 1620, whose wife was sister of the Rev. Robert Parker, "one of the greatest scholars of the English Nation."

James Noyes came to New England because, as Cotton Mather says, "he could not comply with the ceremonies of the Church of England." He had two sons, James and Moses. James, the elder, was Moderator of the Saybrook Synod of 1708, and Moses, himself a member of the Synod, was, according to Dr. Bacon, "a man of great and extensive learning, an excellent Christian, and a judicious divine."

OLD SILLTOWN

He was followed by Samuel Pierpont, in 1722, a young man of great promise, son of Rev. James Pierpont of New Haven, a member of the Saybrook Synod, the one who, it is said, drafted the articles of its platform; who also laid the foundations of a "collegiate school," which afterwards grew into Yale College. "His beautiful and gifted daughter Sarah," as Dr. Bacon says, "a great granddaughter of Thomas Hooker, was like a ministering angel to her husband (the great President Edwards), that wonderful preacher and theologian, whose name is to this day the most illustrious in the history of New England, but who could never have fulfilled his destiny without her."

Such were the family connections of Samuel Pierpont, whose short pastorate of three months in Lyme, closed with one of the most romantic yet sad incidents in history.

In March, 1723, he crossed the Connecticut river to Pettipaug, now Essex, to visit his lady-love living in Middletown. The ferriage was made by the Indians, in canoes, from near Higgins' wood to Ferry-point. Returning, young Pierpont embarked on one of these canoes, and had nearly crossed the river, when a sudden squall rendered the canoe unmanageable among the floating ice, and finally capsized it, when, not being able to swim, he was lost, although his Indian guide saved himself.

This was Lyme's shortest pastorate.

Next came the theologian and revivalist, Jonathan Parsons, in whose writings we learn there were 768 inhabitants in the parish in 1735.

The parish comprised about the same limits as at present, the north society having been formed in 1727, the east parish in 1719—so that, since 1735, this parish has increased in numbers 582.

When Whitefield preached in Boston, in 1740, Parsons, from the strange accounts brought to him of the man and his methods, was inclined to regard him with distrust, and, to satisfy himself, made the journey to New Haven, and afterwards to other places where Whitefield preached, to hear him. Acquaintance with the great preacher undeceived him, and a close friendship sprang up between the two men, which lasted till death.

Tradition says Whitefield came to Lyme to visit Parsons, and preached to the people, gathered beneath, from the great rock in the rear of the present church; and this tradition is probably correct, for he was a great friend of Parsons, who was dismissed from the pastorate of this church in 1745, and followed the fortunes of his friend till his death, which occurred in Parsons' own house, in Newburyport, Mass., on the 30th of September, 1770, and was buried, according to his own desire, in front of the pulpit of the church of which Parsons was the pastor.

A glance at Parsons' itinerary work is interesting. About the time of the "great awakening," several pastors united to invite him to preach for them. He did so. On the 8th of June he preached at Salem; on the 9th, at the north parish of New London. From thence he went to Norwich—thence to Stonington on the 11th. Returning, he preached at Groton on the 12th, Norwich on the 13th; remained there over the Sabbath, when there was a powerful exhibition of contrition and repentance in the congregation. On the 15th he preached to the "new society" in Norwich; on the 16th in

OLD SILLTOWN

New London, where he was invited by Mr. Adams, whose church was divided by the preaching of Davenport, an inflamed orator against everybody, and everything not in accord with himself.

Mr. Parsons endeavored to promote harmony in the churches, and establish the Word in its purity and simplicity.

A singular mania possessed the people of Lyme under his preaching, to publicly confess their sins. We find, for instance, a record of July 11, 1733: one "Thomas Graves offered a confession for breaking the peace and contemning the church, which was accepted;" "Jan. 9, 1732, ———— —————— made and offered a confession for giving way to passion, evil speaking, and intemperate drinking, which was read and accepted." Another confession was made by a woman for abusing her neighbors.

Many confessed the sins of drunkenness, fornication, evil speaking, railing against neighbors, etc., etc., and Mr. Parsons himself read a confession of some dereliction of duty, in which he "severely reflected upon himself."

These confessions being read before the church, the offending members, upon expression of their penitence, were received again into its charity.

Next comes the longest pastorate of the eight, stretching over forty years—the most trying, in many respects, of the years of its existence. They were those between 1746 and 1786—those years that mark the hardships of the French and Indian war, and the struggle of the colonies for freedom from the oppression of the British crown.

This was the pastorate of him whom Bancroft well calls "the incomparable Stephen Johnson."

OLD SILLTOWN

It is the glory of this town and of this society, that while among its pastors it has numbered one whose stirring appeals awoke not only the people of this town to righteousness, but also those of a large section of Connecticut and Massachusetts, through which he itinerated, it has also numbered one whose clear, bold eloquence, coupled, as it was, with a searching, irresistible logic, discovered to the people of New England, God's primal heritage to man, viz.: freedom from oppression, and the inherent right to worship Him, untrammeled by State laws or the decrees of kings.

Nowhere in this New World was the clarion note of a people's freedom more fearlessly or faithfully sounded, than from the pulpit of the First Congregational Church of Lyme.

'Twas fitting that God's minister, while teaching the Fatherhood of God, and the equality of man before him, should proclaim this freedom; and the patriot breast of Johnson, fired with a noble enthusiasm, offered itself to the brunt of regal tyranny, in defending and encouraging the liberties of the colonies.

The next longest pastorate is that which has so lately closed. Davis S. Brainerd began and ended his ministerial life in this church—a life which was given to the work of quiet upbuilding and strengthening of the kingdom of God. Under his pastorate it was that the church passed through the trials of the late war, and steadily prospered from first to last. He was a finished scholar, found worthy to be enrolled among the Fellows of Yale College, whose faculty testified their deep sorrow at his death by their presence at the funeral. He was a man beloved in his parish, and leaves blessed memories behind him.

THE CHURCH MEMBERSHIP.

There is, unfortunately, no record of church membership during the ministry of either Mr. Noyes or Mr. Pierpont—at least none that has come to light as yet; but, from Mr. Parson's time till now, the total membership is 1108.

The largest number added at any one time was during Mr. Parsons' ministry, in 1741, when 148 members were received, and during his entire ministry of fifteen years he received 288 persons into the church. This was the period of religious awakening.

During Mr. Johnson's ministry of forty years, there were added to the church 204 members. This was the exciting period of civil and political commotion; it is marked by the finger of war in all its length. There was no special religious awakening during these forty years of colonial struggle, but a steady, slow growth throughout.

In 1817, during Mr. Rockwell's ministry—in the year when the present meeting-house was finished—there were 82 members received.

In 1832, under Mr. Colton, there were 23 additions.

During Mr. Brainerd's ministry of thirty-five years, there were 265 additions. The largest number received in any one of these years was in 1858, when 61 persons were added to the church.

Since January, this year, there have been added to the church 28 members—the present total active membership being 148.

Thus it will be seen, the years of special interest were 1741, 1817, 1832, 1858, and the present—years which marked a religious interest in all the country. 1876 is but half gone;

may we hope that it will not close without witnessing large additions to the church of Christ, here and elsewhere, of such as shall be saved?

A few interesting notices in regard to the membership, I will cite in passing. In 1740, the Society appointed a committee to "seat men and their wives together," thus in the year of the "great awakening" the old, senseless custom of separating husbands and wives in church, was broken up.

In 1798, the Society set apart the fore seats in the meeting-house for the use of "men over 72 years of age, and women over 64." In reading such a society vote as this, the inquiry naturally suggests itself, where are the aged men and women now-a-days?

We are apt to think there was a larger percentage of these venerable ones in those days than now. Perhaps there was. Yet, on the Centennial 4th of July, there was one man on the grounds, entering heartily into the spirit of the day, whose age is 86.

Besides him, there were a number who are past 80, while those fathers and mothers present aged between 70 and 80 years might easily be mistaken, from their youthful bearing, for men and women in the prime instead of in the decline of life.

It seems as though this air of the mountains and verdant plains mingled with the sea breezes has a wonderful influence in preserving the buoyancy of life. Facts seem to warrant the saying ascribed to Baron Von Humboldt, that the healthiest district in the United States is the stretch of coast from the Connecticut river to Narragansett bay. Ponce DeLeon, in his search for the fountain of perpetual youth, was seven hundred miles too far south, when he entered the everglades of Florida. He never would have made the fatal mistake of entering behind "death's curtains" in Florida, if his brigantine had coasted along our shores.

Our mothers in the olden time braved the cold of winter, to enter a church unheated. They carried with them their brass foot-warmers, and ever as they were cooled, had them replenished with fresh coals from the neighboring fire-places.

Stoves were first introduced into the church in 1829, when the stove-pipes were run out of the windows. Not without opposition, however, were the stoves admitted, yet the people seem readily to have become reconciled to an innovation which soon proved itself a blessing.

It is not well to make a vain parade of our ancestry, even though it be noble; nor to speak boastingly of our antecedents before strangers; yet, in the family, it is proper and beneficial to recount the worthy deeds of our immediate predecessors, and to speak in praise of memorable men, if at the same time we inculcate the principles upon which their lives were founded, and exhort the hearers to emulate them.

Inasmuch then, as it is in the family, let me recall to you the fact that many worthy and honorable men have sat in the councils of this church.

In the meetings of the Society, and serving on its executive committees, we read the names of those whom the State and the whole country delighted to honor. Men whose names are linked with the *best* of modern times.

That the race of noble bloods is extinct, we cannot for a moment believe, but alas! alas! they are very much hidden in the background of private life. Let our prayer and our

OLD SILLTOWN

endeavor be to bring them to the light, that they may take the active part in our politics that their fathers' did.

And here let me urge those who are just entering upon manhood's duties to heed the lives of these men of old, these giants of worth and of work, whose deeds beautify history's page; let me urge you to emulate them. The lesson of the past will be lost to us, and our rehearsal of its worthy deeds will be vain parade, except we profit by it in shaping our lives according to the pattern displayed. Oh! let not the story of the past be fruitless. But let the seeds of honesty, integrity of purpose, and virtue take deep root in your hearts and spring forth in fruit, such that the coming time may recount with pride, and say to the children of that day, as we say to ours, strive to imitate the virtues and the activities of the fathers.

During the 183 years of this church's life, it has been officered by eighteen deacons, elected for life. These officers, no less than the pastors, have contributed to the permanent welfare and prosperity of the church by their uprightness of character, and the wisdom and justice of their dealings.

OUTLINE HISTORY.

As rapidly now as I may, I will sketch the outline of the church's life.

When the country was almost an impenetrable wilderness from Saybrook to Boston, and the Western Nehantic Indians associated with the remnant of the once powerful tribe of Pequots, held this whole stretch of coast as their own peculiar property, and the different tribes from the interior came yearly down to the beach to feast upon clams and fish and bathe in the waters of the Sound, crossing the country on the top of the ridge known as Meeting-house hills.

When these dusky warriors battled with each other, and especially, with the white man whom they regarded as an unwarranted intruder, then it was that a party of resolute men crossed the Great River and formed a settlement here. Then it was that the pioneer preacher, Moses Noyes, ministered to them in the little log meeting-house on the hill, and after 27 years of labor, formed the First Congregational Church of Lyme.

By the laws of Connecticut, the church Society was authorized to tax the people for its support, and empowered to *collect* said taxes before the courts. There seems to have been no trouble about the collection of these taxes until the year 1738, when the Society excepted from its levy "all those persons called Baptists."

At what time the Baptists were here first in any strength, it is difficult to determine, but about the year 1727 Mr. Noyes was much troubled by the preaching of their peculiar tenets here, and conferred with Cotton Mather of Boston, *who came to Lyme* at that time, in regard to it, and they jointly held some discussion with the Baptists, who, however, continued to increase, and were exempted in 1738 from taxation to support the Congregational Church.

Religious liberty began to dawn in the colonies, and the right of their own form or method of worship seems to have been easily and gracefully granted to the Baptists in Lyme, by the Congregationalists, who were then the dominant sect.

In 1792, we see a still greater advance of religious liberty. Heretofore, a tax had been levied to support the ministry, but in this year the pews of the church were sold for this purpose.

The idea was, that only those who enjoyed the privilege should be obliged to pay for the Gospel. But such was the effect of the good old training of families in religious ways, that the church was crowded, and the new method of supporting the ordinances gained in favor each year, although it was some time before the formal levy of a tax perished from sight.

One important epoch in the history of this church was that of the "great awakening," in 1740, to which time we can look back with pride and pleasure, as we recognize in the pastor, Parsons, one of the *great* preachers of that great day.

The next great period of the church's history is that of the Revolution.

Into that struggle this church entered, with clear knowledge as to its probable hardships; but the men who had planted the standard of Christ in the face of a savage, opposing nation, were not the ones to draw back, or to yield their liberties.

This Society gave to the Continental Army officers and men freely, and among them was one of the four celebrated Connecticut fighting chaplains.

It is interesting and instructive to glance at the financial condition of the country at that time, as displayed by our Society records. The depreciation of the currency of the country, after the late War of the Rebellion, has been lamented by some people in the most extravagant terms, they freely asserting that no parallel could be found in history. The fact is, it was as nothing compared with the depreciation of the old bills of credit issued during the French and Indian War, and, especially, with the depreciation of the paper money of the Revolution.

We find that this Society paid its pastor, in 1782, *twenty-five dollars,* in these bills of credit, for every one dollar of "lawful money" due to him, so that a dollar of that depreciated currency was worth just *four cents.*

Another item of interest is this. In 1776, silver was worth two dollars per ounce. It is now worth *one* dollar per ounce. It has shrunk in value, in the last hundred years, just one-half, and, at the present rate of production, it looks as though it would shrink at least ten times as much in the next hundred years.

The next period was one of peace and retrenchment of expenses, broken in upon by that ripple of trouble—the War of 1812.

In 1751, wharfs were built on the Lieutenant river, near the bridge, for the landing of the ships engaged in the West India trade, whose cargoes were stored in large warehouses built on the shore; but, up to the close of the Revolution, our merchantmen were constantly harassed upon the ocean, after which, however, Lyme was a thriving mart of trade. Wealth poured into the town, not only from this source, but also from the great transatlantic passenger lines of ships, many of whose captains were natives of Lyme, who adorned their town with beautiful and commodious dwellings, in some of which their children live; in others, they *themselves* (having laid down the burden of active life) are now spending a well-earned time of quiet and repose.

The next period was one when the tocsin of war again aroused the people into bustling activity. This time it was not a foreign foe who invaded our coasts, but one of those internal retchings and contortions which a nation, working out its liberties, must undergo, shook the States from sea to sea.

With a quick patriotism, worthy of any time, the people ran the Stars and Stripes to the masthead; and, as of yore, this Society supplied men and money to the government to sustain the shock of war. She sent men who, by their valor, earned the shoulder-straps on the field; and she gave a counsellor to the nation, whose heart was so true, whose judgment so clear, that his merits have been publicly recognized by all the people.

And now is the time of peace once more. Like a ship on the sea, buffeting with the waves, and anon gliding over crystal waters, again being tossed in the hurricane, weathering the gales, and sailing, once more, the smooth sea, so this Society, born in the lap of struggle, has sustained the shock of every trial that has shaken the country for the past 200 years; and, constant to the truth, in whose name it was organized, has steadily triumphed over every obstacle and reverse, and stands, today, a united brotherhood.

Disruptions have, for a time, occurred to mar the harmony of its peace; but forgivings and forgettings, and submerging of personal feelings in the common central love to Christ our Lord, have made us *one* people—*an inseparable church.*

The bond of union, in the past, has been Christ and his love. Shall it not be the bond for ever?

Shall the heroism of the fathers, their devotion to their country, to their families, to their God, die with the record? Forbid it, Almighty God!

OLD SILLTOWN

Shall we not reproduce to the world, by the help of God, what was noble and true in them, and give to future history a record as unimpeachable as that of the past?

END OF DR. CARY'S DISCOURSE

OLD SILLTOWN

PRESENT DAY REPLICA OF OLD LYME FIRST CONGREGATIONAL CHURCH.
   On July 3rd 1904, the church erected in 1817 was burned to the ground and many of the surrounding elms were thus destroyed, The church was re-erected in the course of the of the suceeding two years. The illustrations in this book show the old original church and the new replica as well.

RECORD OF THE PASTORATE

FROM SERMON OF REV. D. S. BRAINERD, JULY 1ST, 1866

Names.	Birthplace.	Educated.	Settled.	Dismissed.	Deaths.	Length of Pastorate.	Age.
Moses Noyes	Newbury, Mass.	Harvard, 1659	1693		Nov. 9, 1729	28 years	86
Samuel Pierpont	New Haven.	Yale, 1718.	Dec. 10, 1722		Mar. 15, 1723	3 months	22
Jonathan Parsons	Springfield, Mass.	Yale, 1729.	1730 or 1731	1745			
Stephen Johnson	Newark, N. J.	Yale, 1743.	Dec. 10, 1746		Nov. 8, 1786	40 years	62
Edward Porter	Farmington.	Yale, 1786.	Feb. 24, 1790	Sept. 19, 1792			
Lathrop Rockwell	Lebanon.	Dartmouth, 1789.	Jan. 15, 1794		Mar. 14, 1828	34 years	59
Chester Colton	West Hartford.	Yale, 1804.	Feb. 12, 1829	June 30, 1840		11 years	
Davis Smith Brainerd	Haddam.	Yale, 1834.	June 31, 1841		Apr. 30, 1875	34 years	61

The following pages are for the purpose of making personal memorandum concerning traditions or incidents in connection with the SILL family, thus preserving them in condensed and permanent form.

I